Thrive GIRL, *Thrive!*

From Visionary
Dr. Marsie Ross
The Women's Self Care Crusader

Published EdLyn Press
Washington, DC

Table of Contents

Thrive GIRL, Thrive!

A Woman's Guide for Abundant Mental, Emotional and Spiritual Wellbeing

Thrive Girl, Thrive!

Library of Congress Cataloging-in-
Publication Data is available upon request

ISBN 978-10-87037-30-1

Printed in the United States of America

**For your FREE Self-Care Guide visit
www.HealthyandHappyCoaching.com**

**For information on how to nourish what you
love visit
www.EdLynEssentials.com**

Dedication

This body of work is dedicated to every woman who ever

felt lost, abandoned, overwhelmed, and unworthy.

It's time to believe the truth about your life and purpose...

You are not alone!

You are already a conqueror!

You have already been granted the permission to

<u>THRIVE</u>!

And don't ever, ever, ever forget it!

From Visionary
Dr. Marsie Ross

Permission to Thrive!

Women's health has become a bit of an obsession for me since I turned 40. You see, that was when my life, my beautiful, "successful" life, fell apart. When I look back on that version of me, I see she was all smoke and mirrors. From the outside you would think I was living the dream. I had it all. The man. The money. The job. The 2.5 kids. But inside? Empty. Overwhelmed. Resentful. Afraid. What they don't tell you about the women's anthem "Fake it till you make it." is that if you fake it for too long, you will lose yourself and everything you hold dear. You see, what they don't share is the price for faking it, hiding it, fearing it and avoiding it. The price for me was almost losing my family, my career, and most importantly, myself.

As a woman living in today's fast-paced, ladder climbing, box-checking society, I was driven to get "mine" in every way I could. The first real taste of success came when I graduated from Hampton University with a bachelor's in science and then five years later graduated from, Howard University, another prestigious HBCU, with a doctorate in pharmacy. I was a doctor y'all! In fact, I was the second doctor in my family's known history. I was praised and highlighted at every family gathering, whether on the phone, in an email or in person. I was their shining light. And I loved it!

Check.

Five years after earning my doctorate, I married the love of my life. Now, this was also a big deal because as a professional in her mid-30's most of my family waited with bated breath for me to tie the knot. My mother and father grew more impatient to become grandparents as the years rolled by. I would discard suitors for even the slightest infraction. The truth is, I loved my single life! I loved the freedom of it. I just could not find a mate that could keep my attention. Now, don't get me wrong. My journey also included a few heartbreaks. But I often chalked them up to the game and was happy to just keep on playing it. I had no fear of my biological clock or marrying a man just for status or because my friends were getting married and having babies. Until I met him…

Tall, dark, handsome, kind *and* arrogant. Why Lord? But when I fell in love, I knew he was "the one" for me. The one that was my match. The one I would be faithful to and the one who I would even share my social security number with! That was huge for me. Trusting someone with my heart and money.

In April 2006, we exchanged vows in front of 200 of my parents' closest friends. After I kept them waiting so long, my parents were determined to live up to the "our wedding, you're married" concept.

Check.

We planned to wait a bit before we started our family, but we all know how a cold winter's night and a few margaritas can change all of that! So, as fate would have it, seven months after our wedding (oops!) we would welcome our first son, Jayson. And to my parents' delight, almost two years to the day later, we would welcome our second son, Jonah.

Check. Check.

With our growing family, we also grew in our square footage. Our 5-bedroom, 4-bathroom estate was a sight to see. We did tons of renovating and decorating early. If anyone has ever been through this process, you know how grueling it can be. And if you've been through it with a husband, a toddler, an infant, and a puppy, then I'm sure you understand how taxing it could be. But when you're chasing the American Dream, you don't stop to think about the price of admission. Several months after moving in to my dream home, the walls were painted perfectly, the floors, countertops, bathrooms, and in-law suite were all updated, furnished, and ready for a magazine spread.

Check. Check and Check.

Now, this is my life on speed play. Let's take a minute to digest the super evolution of me. In the span of six years, I went from college graduate to a doctor and corporate professional. In just two lightening years later I went from being single (and ready to mingle) to becoming a wife, a mom, twice, a puppy mom and the co-owner of a newly removed large single-family home.

Wow! Within a few years, these boxes I've been checking started to feel like cages.

Can you relate?

Has your life ever felt like it wasn't yours? That you are just existing to serve others? That you lost "you" along the way?

Well, I sure did! But because my glasshouse was so pretty and shiny, I could not share the turmoil openly. I would share it passive-aggressively. But openly? No. I would share it with resentment. But honestly? Never. The ugly truth was too much for me to admit. I was feeling overwhelmed and living as a stranger in my skin.

Seven years into our marriage, we were almost like strangers. We exchanged pleasantries, and he tried to connect with me, but the "me" he married was buried under all of my to-do lists and unmet expectations. We had the obligatory sex and exchanged hello and goodbye kisses, but the passion that once lived and breathed between us was a faint whisper. The connection of togetherness was gone. He would call me on the phone to see how my day was going, and I would offer him only impatience and disdain. I was angry and frustrated constantly, and all of those feelings were being dumped on him regularly. I was not equipped to process my true feelings in an honest and authentic way.

I was too busy trying to "Fake it till I made it." The problem was, in the faking, I had stopped growing and evolving with my life. My life kept moving on the outside, but internally, my growth was stunted. By trying to be everything for everyone, I stopped being anything for myself. By trying to keep up with my mother's and grandmother's model of a wife, mother, and career women, I became haunted by the fear of failure. What's wrong with me? Why can't I keep my house in order? Why is my son not by potty trained before two years old? Why won't my baby eat more vegetables? Am I a bad mom? Why am I so unfocused at work? Why am I feeling so overwhelmed? Why can't I lose this baby weight with the second baby?

From the outside it was good but inside, all I felt was failure.

But I had the man, money, kids, home, and career. So, what was I missing?

When our relationship came to an impasse my husband and I sought the guidance of a marriage counselor. It was her gentle and sometimes blunt guidance that helped me find my way back to me. She helped me identify the underlining source of the fear of failure. She helped me communicate my needs to my husband in a way that honored both of us and our marriage. He still doesn't keep the house in order the way I want, but after 13 years, I have learned to pick my battles.

People often ask me what changed the course of our relationship. I tell them that I chose to save myself. I often get blank stares at first because for many women and especially mothers, the concept of putting themselves before their man, job, or children feels very, very, very uncomfortable. But it's true. You cannot be the best for anyone until you are the best for yourself.

Here is a simple way to invite passion and purpose back into your life. Ask yourself these three questions. Once you've answered them, I challenge you to answer them again and this time, dig deeper!

- Who am I, and what brings me joy? The key here is to not include (or hide behind) spouse, boyfriend, children or job. Who are YOU! What brings YOU joy!
- How do I feel about myself and why? This is your time to get real. List the good, bad and the ugly
- What area of my life would I like to see flourish? What are the 3 steps I will take to make this happen?

You see, once you realize the power to walk in your truth already exists within you, then you will truly be on a path of abundance. And when I say abundance, I am not even remotely talking about "things." I am a testament that it is easy to have an abundance of things and still not thrive. I am also a testament that you cannot use your children as an excuse to phone your evolution and growth. You and you alone can walk your path. I'll leave you with my favorite quote by Maya Angelou with the hopes that you will understand your purpose was born with you and all you have to do is walk in it!

*"My mission in life is not merely to survive, but to **thrive**;*
And to do so with some passion, some compassion, some
humor, and some style."
~Maya Angelou

About the Visionary

Dr. Marsie Ross empowers and educates women to take charge of their health & happiness. She works with women who are ready to get to the good part of healthy living so they can lead effectively, sustain quality relationships, and live with authentic confidence. As a mother, wife, and CEO, Dr. Marsie knows first-hand the uphill battles women face with sustaining positive body images and maintaining good mental and emotional health. Dr. Marsie is best-selling author and international speaker, Doctor of Pharmacy and Certified Integrative Nutrition Health Coach. Dr. Marsie is known as the "Self-Care Crusader." She is on a mission to build an army of self-care crusaders who embrace self-care without guilt or apology!

Healthy and Happy Coaching

www.HealthyandHappyCoaching.com

EdLyn Essentials www.EdLynEssentials.com

Booking Inquiries: ReadyToThrive@DrMarsie.com

Connect with Dr. Marsie (FaceBook, Instagram, Twitter)

@DrMarsie @EdLynEssentials

Thrive Girl, *Thrive!*

A Woman's Guide for Abundant Mental, Emotional and Spiritual Wellbeing

The Experts

Dr. Celeste Owens
Surrender

Dr. Valeka Moore
Thrive or Die

Surrender
By Dr. Celeste Owens

Some years ago, I happened upon an amazing Master Class video posted by Oprah Winfrey entitled: Surrender. In it, she shared her arduous journey to being cast in the Color Purple. She stated she never wanted anything more than she wanted the Color Purple, but as life would have it, her dream seemed far from reach. The production team had not reached out to her, and when she made a call to the casting director, he told her he had more talented actresses trying out for the part. She was crushed and checked herself into a "fat farm." Incidentally, just when she thought her dream was never to be, a song rose up in her heart: I Surrender All, and as she sang this song out loud, she visualized herself giving it all back to God. In that instant, she received a phone call from Steven Spielberg offering her a part in the movie.

• • •

Although this story might sound far-fetched to some, I, too, have experienced the benefits of surrender time and time again in my own life. I've learned that the simple act of letting go brings about miraculous results.

Surrender is doing God's will, His way. It's also an act of letting go. Not giving up or quitting, but doing your part, then detaching from the outcome and allowing God to do what He desires to do to bring about a great victory for you.

In some circles, my name has become synonymous with the word surrender. Here's why. In 2010 I made a radical career move that changed the course of my life. At that time, I was in private practice as a psychologist, on a national speaking platform, and ministry leader at my church. My life screamed for success. However, defining success simply by accomplishments is not wise. There may come a day when God tells you to leave it all as He did with me.

At a Christmas dinner party, while listening to a couple share the most incredible surrender story I had ever heard--a story of how they left their military careers just before retirement because God told them too--I heard the Holy Spirit whisper to me, you are going to do that too.

Leave everything, and I'll give you further instructions once you do.

I totally thought I heard wrong, and I was more than happy to let Andel decide if I was discerning the voice of God correctly or just plain crazy. But to my surprise when I told Andel what I thought the Holy Spirit had told me to do, he said, "If you think that is God, you need to do it."

With that, I spent the entire year of 2009, leaving everything, and at the top of 2010, I found myself home with 3 degrees and 2 children. For the first 3 months, I spent most of my time questioning God and my decision. I couldn't understand why God would have me go to school for so long to close my practice. I couldn't understand why God would require me to leave the ministry. I couldn't understand why God would suggest I leave my speaking platform after finally getting comfortable with public speaking.

That was the problem as long as I concentrated on the "why me" (victim mindset), the "why, not me" (victor mindset) remained untapped. In order to move from why me to why not me, I needed a complete mental overhaul. I had to become purposeful and contemplative about the thoughts I was allowing yourself to have. I started to examine and challenge my thoughts during that time: *Was my perception of reality true? Had God called me to leave everything so that I would lose my purpose?*

The answer was a resounding NO!

In those moments of uncertainty, I reminded myself that God was for me and He had a magnificent plan for me; that He would never leave me nor forsake me, and great were His thoughts toward me. Once I changed my mindset to match the truth of my existence, my season changed. Once my mindset caught up with my new reality, and I said yes, God then had permission to move on my behalf. Accordingly, that same year, I wrote a book called *The 40-Day Surrender Fast*. That book, birthed from my obedience, has reaped the most incredible fruit. I am now an international speaker, publisher, healer, and the author of 3 books and counting. In fact, *The 40-Day Surrender Fast* has been translated into 2 other languages and has sold over 20,000 copies.

All of this because I surrendered.

Surrender isn't easy, but it's worth it. Getting to a posture of surrender takes effort, pain, and sweat. The process is made remarkably more challenging by our egos, which think it knows best. In fact, it is said that the ego stands for edging God out and as we edge Him out, we back ourselves into a corner because we can't see the future and we don't know what is best for us. We see with limited eyesight and engage our environment from a worldview that is sorely lacking inexperience. King David proclaimed, "How precious are your thoughts about me, O God. They cannot be numbered!" This demonstrates that we serve a God that can be trusted with every aspect of our lives. He wants to do great things if we would only lay our egos aside.

So, in 2009, when God told me to leave everything, He did so with a knowledge of what was to come. In fact, He knows the end from the beginning; His thoughts and plans for you are good, and He makes every decision with eternity in mind. With that said, surrender is what you need to do to live your best life. So, the question becomes, how do you get to and maintain a posture of surrender? In other words, what does surrender look like and how do you do it continually so that you live your best life.

The Flow of God

My life has been one big lesson in surrender. What I know now, that I didn't know then is that God was continually teaching me how to surrender so that I could one day teach others how to do the same.

Surrender is about getting into the flow of God, about knowing His voice and moving as He directs. If we are not accustomed to experiencing God's presence, it is much harder to recognize when He is moving and speaking. However, just because we can't hear Him, doesn't mean He is not speaking. God is always speaking. He speaks through His Word, through other people and even through nature. So, the problem isn't if He is speaking, the problem lies in our ability to hear. Our hearing is hindered by distractions such as busyness, but in order to get into God's flow, we have to invite Him in. There are several ways to do that.

First, in order to get into the flow of God, you must make His business, your business. The Word tells us to seek first His Kingdom and His righteousness, and all these things will be added to us. The problem is that we are seeking our kingdom and we want to advance our own agenda, but when you decide to live a lifestyle of surrender you decide to forego your opinion for that of God's, knowing and trusting that He knows best.

Second, you get into God's flow when you decide to allow His grace to empower you in all you do. I find that so many people are frustrated because they are trying to make things happen in their own strength. I've been there. Take dating. There was a time in my young adulthood that I decided it was time for me to get married. Not because God said it was time, but because all the friends in my social circle were getting married. Comparisons are dangerous. When we compare, we put ourselves in the space of desperation that we were never meant to reside, and from that place of despair, we often acquire the counterfeit of the thing we seek.

God wanted me to marry, but not at the time; I wanted to be married. Timing is everything. So, I had to kiss a few frogs first. Then finally, I got to the end of myself and surrendered my singleness to God. It was a simple prayer, "God, it's okay that I am single, and if I never get married, that's okay too." His grace empowered me to say that prayer and His grace empowered me to enjoy the last 6 months of my singlehood. Yes, you read that correctly, just 6 months after saying that prayer, I met my husband Andel at a wedding, and we have been married for 18 years. It is said that surrender advances and I am living witness that that is a fact.

Thirdly, you get into the flow of God through obedience. So many people don't realize that the first step to living your best life is just to say yes. In 2010, I said yes, and my life changed in the most amazing way. A yes gives God permission to work in and through you.

Saying yes, it isn't easy; it takes courage and faith. Especially when God shows up to say things like, "you are an international healing ministry" while you're still in your family room writing blogs that 50 people at best are reading. But if He said it, He meant it, and He is faithful to perform it.

So, when He said I was an international speaking ministry, although I couldn't see it, I said yes. About 6 months later a friend of mine phoned to say I should get my passport. I didn't waste any time; within 2 weeks I had applied for my passport. That was 2011. Four years would pass before I got my first international speaking engagement. Out of the blue, I received a call from a ministry leader inviting me to speak at his church for both Wednesday night Bible Study and Sunday morning service. Unbeknownst to me, it was an international church in my local area. When I arrived at the church, I was greeted by a host of flags, lining both sides of the sanctuary, flags from every country imaginable. I immediately got excited; I knew in an instant that God was up to something great. I also sensed that from that church, I had been released to international ministry. So, when I get up to speak, I tell the congregation this revelation and the Pastor of the church prays a prayer of confirmation of our release to international ministry.

As God would have it, the next day, I open my email and in it lies a letter from a Bishop in Kenya inviting me to speak at his Pastor and Leaders Conference. I was beyond elated. God had kept His promise. When I announce to the church that Sunday that I had been invited to speak at this conference, the church erupted in praise. Not only that, the Pastor told me she would pay my airfare to the conference.

Faith Over Fear

We serve a mighty God. If you are waiting on Him to move, don't be discouraged. Although the dream may be delayed, if God spoke it, it is not denied. Just continue to hold onto your yes, and before you know it, He will move on your behalf.

Again, surrender is about saying yes to the people, assignments, and things that are assigned to you. Many people avoid saying yes out of fear; fear of the unknown, fear of failure, and even fear of success. However, the truth is that yes opens the door for your best life.

There have been many times I have said yes, despite the fear. My Pastor says that "rather than run from the fear, go in the direction of the fear" knowing that something better is on the other side of your yes. A yes will stretch you outside of what feels comfortable, but I've heard it said that greatness happens outside of the comfort zone. God honors a radical faith. When I left everything in 2010, I did so in a radical act of faith, not knowing what was next. Having faith requires you to move without evidence and surrender your mind and surrender your reason. When you have faith, no scientific support is needed. According to the Bible, faith is the substance of things hoped for and the evidence of things not seen. I often say in order to see the manifestation of things not seen; you have to see it (in your mind) before you see it (with your eyes).

A yes opens doors that would have remained closed had I opted for no. Nearing the end of the completion of my doctorate degree, I was faced with a dilemma--say yes to an internship that was 16 hours by car from my new husband Andel and our home, or forego the internship all together and stay home. At that time, saying yes to the internship seemed risky, scary, and even selfish. However, with my husband's support, I said yes. That yes opened doors I didn't know were possible. One such door was free airfare. Again, by car, I was 16 hours away from my home in Maryland, so in my eyes that limited travel and the number of times I would see Andel that year. However, about the same time, I was accepting the internship God directed by sister to apply for an airline job, and she got it. Upon learning that I had accepted the internship in Chicago, she offered me flying privileges in her husband's stead. I was home almost every weekend at no cost.

The internship was also risky because the American Psychological Association did not approve of the program. I would venture that 99% of psychology graduate students would not take an internship that was not APA approved, however, because the internship sounded tailored made for me, I took it anyway, and before I graduated, they received their accreditation.

One other unexpected blessing of this internship was dissertation help. For me, the most challenging part of completing the dissertation was the statistical portion of the paper; I was struggling badly. At my internship, a woman befriended me who I later learned got a perfect score on the math portion of the GRE and loved statistics. She helped me to complete the dissertation, and not only that I understood statistics well enough to defend my dissertation successfully. All this was made possible because I said yes!

A yes will stretch you but understand this; a yes will work for your good and your expansion. Playing it safe will keep you living a mediocre life that amounts to a fraction of what you could have been had you said yes.

Don't let your fear get in the way of God's best life for you. Remember, God responds to faith and will move mountains for you if you would only believe.

Surrender Brings Out the True You

Lastly, surrender allows you to come face-to-face with yourself. It allows you to also know the truth--that you are a creation of the King and made in His image to perform incredible feats. I don't care what you have experienced in life, you are the apple of His eye, and He has plans for you that will blow your mind.

I didn't always believe that; that I was special to Him and placed on this earth for a very special purpose. It was a while before I believed that no one could beat me at being me. If you are challenged in the area of knowing your worth, let me offer this advice. Get in God's face, read His Word, and ask Him to change your thinking.

For so many years, I didn't know my worth, and because of that, I lived beneath my privilege. However, God created environments for me to grow. Some people call them wilderness experiences. They are not pleasant, but they are necessary. It is in the wilderness that I learned to surrender everything to Him; my hopes, my dreams, my everything. It is only in the giving back that true transformation and advancement can take place.

Whatever you believe about yourself that is not the truth about you, send it back to the pit from which it came. I used to believe I wasn't good enough or smart enough. I used to compare myself to others, but that year, I was on an internship in Chicago that changed my life. It was in that place of isolation and solitude that I experienced healing. Don't fear silence, instead surrender to it and find your peace.

In Chicago, I developed a practice of spending time with God in the morning, and a decade later, it is still the way I start my day and the way I live my day. In fact, throughout the day, I surrender my being to God, my decisions, my everything. Even when things don't appear to be going your way, remember that all things work for your good and that He loves you very much.

It's your time to thrive! Don't let anything get in your way. Find yourself, live His truth, and you will prosper in every way imaginable.

About the Author

Dr. Celeste Owens is a speaker, a psychologist by training, a trauma specialist, and a Certified Natural Health Professional specializing in the promotion of spirit, mind, and body wellness. She is also the author of *The 40-Day Surrender Fast*. She and her husband Andel travel the globe teaching the philosophy of surrender which she says is simply doing God's will, His way, all the time!

Dr. Celeste Owens Ministries, www.drcelesteowens.com

Booking inquiries: info@drcelesteowens.com

Connect with Dr. Celeste on all social media platforms @DrCelesteOwens

Thrive or Die
By Dr. Valeka Moore

I tried to stop, but it happened so fast. I wanted to bring it back up, but it was lodged in my throat, blocking my airway.

Have you ever felt like you were dying?

That was my first experience with the thought that I could die. I was about 18 years old, sitting in a church service, sucking on an atomic fireball jawbreaker candy. And before I knew it, I was choking on it. My first inclination was to leave out without making a scene or even being noticed because even in a moment as terrifying as this, it was my norm to try to blend in and not bring attention to myself. Then it hit me. I didn't need to hide this. Just in case the situation continued to go wrong, I needed someone to know what was taking place. As I was quickly leaving out of the sanctuary, I motioned to my mother, who was standing in the back. I was able to gain her attention but didn't wait for her to come. Once I made it into the hallway, I bent over and attempted to bring it up again. It didn't matter what I had to do or how it happened. Whether I threw up all over the steps or whatever the embarrassing outcome may have been. I just knew I needed to get it up and out. And thank God, this time it worked! Although it was a little hard to swallow for the next day or so, it was OK because I was alive. But trust and believe, to this day, I have never eaten a fireball again!

6 years later...

I felt drained. I could literally feel the life leaving my body. I was dying. Oh, my God! I can't be dying... All I knew is that I had to fight to live. I was 24 years old and had just given birth to my first child — a beautiful, seven-pound baby girl. After nearly 21 hours of labor, which resulted in a cesarean, I finally got to lay my eyes on the little person that had been invading body for the past nine months. I was so excited! And then just like that, I felt like I was losing my breath. In a split second, I felt like I was slipping away. How was it possible that I had just experienced one of the most treasured moments of a woman's life, and I was going to die?

This could not be real. After realizing that I was wearing myself out by fighting out loud, by demanding water and demanding to be removed from the operating room so I could have water, which of course did not work because the doctor was still in the middle of stitching me back up, I decided that I needed to fight differently. I decided that I needed to breathe and allow myself to relax. It wasn't easy, but see, when you have a strong will to live, you make the necessary adjustments that give you the best chances of doing so. Thankfully, almost 15 years later, I am here to tell you about that scary incident. One thing I knew after that day was that I never wanted to feel that way again.

Isn't it funny how we say we never want to experience or encounter a thing, especially if we have already had one go around, yet we put ourselves directly in the line of fire? The very situations that have the propensity to create an outcome that we don't desire. What causes this insanity? Do we just ignore or turn a blind eye to the signs? Do we think that it will never happen to us or can't happen again? Like we have some type of immunity. Is it possible that we simply don't recognize what is taking place right within our very lives? Is it possible that we are in the cycle and don't know how to get out? Whatever the cause, if we don't take inventory and make the necessary adjustments, we will continually find ourselves in the same harmful, unhealthy, and sometimes traumatic states. I'm not speaking of the fact that after that slightly traumatic delivery, I have since then had two additional children. Actually, I'm not speaking in a physical sense much at all. Often, we will give physical factors much consideration and set out to make beneficial adjustments. But I'm eluding to those things which are mental in nature.... or at least starts off that way. Because just know that unaddressed mental/ emotional conditions will likely cause physical issues. They work hand in hand.

My wakeup call was in November 2013. It was during that time that we begin to set goals and make plans for the new year. Just like becoming a mother, years before, I was in the process of entering another monumental time in my life. After years of entertaining the idea of entrepreneurship, I was three months from stepping out and birthing the vision of starting my own therapy practice. God had given me this vision 15 years prior. On top of that, I was a wife to an amazing husband and mother of three awesome children. I was a doctoral student, and the call to ministry was also on my life. I was the daughter of pastors. My wardrobe was fly. I wore 4-5 inch heels to work on most days. My hair was laid. I drove a fly car. My work and my work ethic spoke for themselves. Before deciding to resign, I was up for a big promotion. Life was great, right? Everything was lining up perfectly, right? I should have been feeling on top of the world excited, right? Well... I said everything was *fine, OK, good.* You know all of the general responses that we give when asked how we're doing. This is what I had even convinced my own self. Until that one day, in November, that I sat in my office, at the organization in which I was working, at the time. That day for some reason, I seemed to be the only person in the office. It was quiet — the perfect setting to do some good thinking. The only thing is, my mind was filled with unwelcomed thoughts. Unwanted. But definitely not undetected. I have to admit that for quite some time, even before this moment, these very thoughts had attempted to surface. But what do we often do when we don't want to deal with something? We push it down. We sweep it under the rug. We try to act as though it's not even there. It just seems easier. It will eventually go away and resolve itself. Right? Wrong! So wrong. In an instant, emotion took over. They came up like a flood. I realized how drained I was feeling. I felt as though I was aging by the second. I once again felt like I was dying... Only this time, unrelated to a physical circumstance. Although the emotion consumed me so quickly, unlike the previous two situations, the "feeling of loss of life" wasn't sudden. The feeling of losing my breath hadn't gone unnoticed. It had just been ignored. I had fought hard to suppress things for months. Years even. Being completely transparent, I'll just admit that it dated back to childhood. And now in one moment, all that I had held in and pushed down and fought against dealing with, throughout most of my life was coming to the surface. The burden had become way too heavy. I was 33 years old, and I was allowing myself to die before my time. I'm not one to make new year resolutions, but one thing that I knew for sure, right then and there was that I could no longer continue on the way that I had been. I needed to use that same mentality that I had with the fireball. Some things needed to come up, and I had to allow them to do just that. Just as I had done, following the delivery of my precious daughter, I needed to begin to fight in a different and more effective way.

Now, let's top it off with the fact that I was a therapist, a mental health therapist, who worked with clients nearly every day, for years, helping them to make changes in their lives that would release them from a burden, hardship, and brokenness. I supported them with implementing the tools that enabled them to live their best-blessed life. Their dream lives even. And here I was, for years, going against everything that I had been encouraging others to do. The outside image exuded boss lady, who had it all together, while on the inside, it was all falling apart. I was living out that saying, "Those who can't do teach." Or maybe it was more, "Do what I say, not what I do." Either way, it was absolutely ridiculous and was not helpful to anyone. It was undoubtedly time for a change. That's where my process began. It was time for a huge mental shift. And it needed to begin with a mental detox. My life depended on it, as well as the lives of those who were connected to me in some way or another. I was getting ready to elevate my career, and that called for me to elevate in my mind and my health. And this time when I said to myself that I never want to feel that way again, I meant it deeply.

I wanted to make sure I lived my life fully and freely according to the purpose and plans that God had for me and not according to insecurities, disappointments, and the ideals of others, that had been weighing me down and destroying the person that I had been created to be.

So, I did the work, and it was a process. It was a journey of reflecting, releasing, refocusing, resetting, and replenishing. It didn't happen overnight, and I didn't figure it out right away, but I was committed to the process. I uncovered so much and began to unload. Sometimes we get consumed by guilt or worry about what others will think or say. But my stage of reflecting showed me that was one of my main hindrances. I permitted myself to unload; to release. To come from behind the mask. Yes, I had maintained a great image, but I hadn't been truly living. I was only existing and surviving and going with the flow. Now freedom was finally taking place. And ever since, I have been on the journey to live fully.

When I started my business a few months later, my targeted client populations were youth and families. I had a strong background working with this population, and I loved it. It just felt right, and I was so excited about it. I wasn't opposed to working with many populations, as I had worked with most populations at some point during my career. The children came. The families came. Couples came. Men came. But most of all, the women came — more and more women. Every time I looked up; I had a new woman client. And what I found is that I truly enjoyed working with women. There was something very familiar about many of these women. They reminded me of me. They reminded me of me in the very place that I had been in, just a few months before. These were women from all walks of life — many in leadership roles. Brilliant women. Powerful women. Wives. Mothers. Executives. Entrepreneurs. Ministers. Pastors. First ladies. Educators. Military. Students. Even wellness professionals. They had their differences, but most shared a very interesting similarity — lack Of Proper Self Care. As I would sit and listen to their situations, which usually consisted of them being in a place of transition or like my situation, realizing that they could no longer continue on as they had been, I would ask them about their self-care habits. Most of the time, I would hear responses such as "What do you mean?" "What is Self-Care?" "There is no time for that." Or they would look at me like I had three heads. And after five years in private practice working with women, a population that I had no idea would dominate my clientele; I still receive the same responses today. A lot of the women do not go as drastic to say that they feel like they are dying, but most will at least admit that they feel as though they are drowning.

Isn't it interesting how things come full circle? Years before I was in the very same mindset of these wonderful women. But now after digging deeper, going through my own journey and discovering the importance of self-care, I am a better me. I am a better wife and mother. I am a better therapist. I can educate and provide tools to my clients from a place of genuine understanding of their mindset and insight on strategies for transformation. I have always been passionate about helping others achieve positive mental health. However, I know that there is a difference between passion and purpose. I believe that we all have a purpose and people assigned to the purpose that was placed within us, at the time we were created. Although my breakthrough was a challenging encounter, it was very necessary, for me to impactfully operate within the purpose and authenticity. And it feels phenomenal.

Now that is the life that I want to see for every one of my beautiful sisters. In fact, I speak life over you right now! And when I say *life,* I don't mean it arbitrarily. I mean a life of freedom, power, and significance. Sometimes when we consider the idea of self-care, we feel that we cannot entertain it because we cannot fit it in. We feel that what makes our lives significant are the deeds that we do. It feels overwhelming to actually take time for us. But I always say to my clients and others "if you are unable to fit yourself in your own life, then your life is too full" and some adjustments must be made. You must make time for you. At if you dare, *take* time for you. Remember, it doesn't have to take long. It just has to take place. Here are a few simple tips to help you jumpstart your journey to truly live and thrive.

Take a Break and Breathe

I think we sometimes take for granted the power of what we consider to be a natural part of living. Breathing is integral to living. It characterizes our humanity. And some days as life is happening, our breathing is affected, and we don't even realize it, because we are so consumed with the happenings of the day — all of the things that we just have to get done. I encourage you to take at least three breaks daily to just stop, close your eyes, and focus on your breathing. Take three deep breaths, then focus on your breathing, returning back to its normal pace. Repeat as needed. Deep breathing is a relaxing agent and also helps with recognizing and neutralizing difficult emotions.

Assess Your True Feelings

Generally, when we are asked how we are doing, our responses consist of "I'm fine." "I'm good." "I'm OK." However, sometimes, these statements are far from the true nature of how we are feeling. I encourage you to set aside time for yourself daily or weekly to honestly assess how you are feeling. Identify the emotions you have felt during the day or week. Which ones are lingering and need to be addressed? Once you can identify how you truly feel, you can then figure out what you need or need to do differently. Permit yourself to do just that.

Release

Throughout life, we consume so much. But a lot of what we take in is not meant for us to carry. Those situations, people, and things can create an emotional burden. Are you holding on to anything that you have had difficulty letting go? One way of dealing with our emotions is by letting them out. One way of letting our emotions out is by getting them out of our heads. I encourage you to begin a therapeutic process with a professional counselor or coach that can support and guide you in determining what needs to be released and effective strategies for doing so. However, sometimes before we actually talk things out, it is easier to transfer them from our minds to the paper. Journaling helps us to organize the clutter in our minds, focus our thoughts, and prepare to express our thoughts and feelings out loud. Another helpful and very human way of releasing is by allowing the physiological responses to surface. Sometimes we feel the need to "be strong" and resist vulnerability. When dealing with difficult emotions, remember that it is perfectly alright and natural to cry, even scream and yell. Emotions are energy, and when we release them, we feel so much better. The next time you are alone, just take a moment and let it all out.

Be Blessed, Brilliant, and Thrive my sister!!!

About the Author

Dr. Valeka Moore is a devoted wife and mother. She is an award-winning entrepreneur and the CEO/ founder of Brilliant One Unlimited and Empowerment Thru Expression. Dr. Valeka is a life and business coach, speaker, therapist, prophetic minister and the author of the Mental Detox For The Brilliant Woman Leader, Visionary Author of The Breaking To Brilliance anthology series, in addition to other empowering book collaborations. Affectionately known as Dr. V., this *Transformation Activator*, is passionate about assisting individuals through processes of breakthrough and healing, and empowers amazing women leaders, to shift from being stuck, confused and frustrated through strategies to transform their minds, businesses and lives, as they fully embrace and activate the next level of their God-given purpose and brilliance!

Brilliant One Unlimited
Empowerment Thru Expression
www.drvalekamoore.com
Booking inquiries: info@drvalekamoore.com Connect with Dr. Valeka (Facebook, Instagram, LinkedIn)
@DrValekaMoore

The Authors

- ❖ ***<u>Ashley Crews</u>*** Breaking Barriers
- ❖ ***<u>Christine Green</u>*** Traveling Through the Human Heart
- ❖ ***<u>Dr. Cortesha Cowan</u>*** Your Vision is Not Substantiated by *Their* Opinions. Don't You Dare Abort It
- ❖ ***<u>Dr. Lisa Greene Henderson</u>*** Balance…Keeping it Together and Finding Your Rhythm as a Mother
- ❖ ***<u>Dr. Leslie Hodge</u>*** From Rejection to Reflection! See Beyond the Moment
- ❖ ***<u>Meagan Tamara Copelin, MBA</u>*** Mental Health and the Empowered Woman
- ❖ ***<u>Meg Nocero, Esq.</u>*** Butterflies, Come Alive to The Beauty of Your Dreams!
- ❖ ***<u>Makeeta House</u>*** Loving Yourself with Self-Love
- ❖ ***<u>Dr. Tiffany Taft</u>*** More Than a Womb
- ❖ ***<u>Cathy Upshire</u>*** Power Boosters

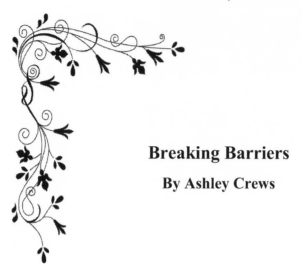

Breaking Barriers

By Ashley Crews

Growing up, I was always a head strong and very aware child. I remember my mom always said that because of my independent attitude, she never really felt the need to worry about me. Her confidence gave me inspiration as an adult to stay strong, focused, and consistent with my goals and achieve everything I wanted in life. As the oldest of my mother's four children and the middle child of my father's nine children, it wasn't always easy for me. As a child, I watched my family endure many struggles that would easily break any individual, but I knew early on that I had to develop a different type of skin to survive. I know that it is my tough skin that gave me the strength to survive my challenging and often unstable childhood. When I say "struggles," I truly mean like the number of times I had to pick up and start over again. Both of my parents suffered from drug addiction, and that ultimately had a ripple effect in my life. I have been in the foster care system, a victim of molestation and moved in and out of homeless shelters. All of this was more than enough for any young woman to give up on herself and to hold anger and resentment toward her parents. But as an adult, I try to remember that nobody is perfect and that my parents always did the best they could to raise their children. One of the best things my mother could have done was send us to church with our grandmother every Sunday.

My grandmother was, and still is, very faithful to her religion, and she showed me how important it is to believe in something bigger than myself. I still remember the name of the church we attended, "Gates of Pearl Holy Baptist." I loved the name because it was such a beautiful and stately name for a church. Although it was a small church, the name made it sound so prominent. The good thing about a small church is that everyone felt like family to us. The not so good thing is that everyone knew my family's story. But that's not so bad because whenever we visited, the whole church often prayed over us. They were my first church family. I think having that support also played a huge role in my ability to stay strong for my family. Even in my lowest of times, I always believed in the Most High and His ability to create breakthroughs, and that unresolved trauma will not stay buried for long. After going through so much pain and suffering growing up, I felt so bitter and angry. It wasn't until after college that I finally started to accept my childhood and let go of my past hurts. I was ashamed for a very long time, and I limited myself from being open about it so that no one could judge me. Even writing this story now, I get chills because I am exposing the truths of my life. As I grew into an adult, I realized that the choices I made bared a huge impact on my relationship with my family, friends, and men. I was so harsh and judgmental, and I did not like the fruit that these emotions bared in my life. I became less judgmental when I realized that I wasn't the only one struggling in life. I used to think I was the only one who knew about life's struggles. It wasn't until I connected with a friend who had a similar story like mine that I realized there was nothing making me so special that I'd be the only one with a story. Everyone has a story. I am no longer ashamed of my humble beginnings or the ugliness of my past because it all made me the woman I am today! Proud, confident, and strong.

But it is also important to look at your past in order to understand yourself and to make peace with who you are in the present. When I think back on my childhood, there were signs all along guiding me toward who I would grow up to be and what would fuel my passion for success and help me Break Down the Barriers of life. As an active child, I was drawn to movement. Dance very quickly become an outlet for me when I was feeling down or frustrated by an unexpected move or family drama. I started dancing at age 7 and fell in love with how it allowed me to express myself and bond with people who became like family to me. I loved and still, love how my body moves in dance. This outlet brought me so much joy and helped me build relationships that I have to this day. Have you ever needed an outlet from frustrations in your life? Did you have the opportunity to use it? How did it make you feel?

My other passion was hair! My mom did not have any talent for styling my hair, and after being teased and tormented so many times at school, I started experimenting with doing it myself. It's never fun to get teased by your peers, but this turned out to be something that worked in my favor. As a creative spirit, doing hair allowed me to explore my creative side. There were times my cousin would braid my sister's hair, and I would be mesmerized watching her from start to finish. It wasn't until I was 9 years old that I attempted to braid my hair and did very good on my first try.

Styling hair was also another outlet for me, keeping my focus on something positive while helping others.

I am thankful that I was able to dance and learn how to style hair because it taught me discipline and how to make smart choices for my future. I knew I had to go to school, get a degree that would hopefully land me a secure, well-paying job so that I could always be a provider for myself and my future family. I didn't and still don't want to put my family through anything that I have experienced.

When I entered high school, I joined an afterschool program called The Harlem Children's Zone. This program changed my life! Not only did it change my views on the importance of education, but it paid the participants to receive tutoring, college mentoring, and preparation classes. I stayed in this program until I graduated from college. They were so involved in my success that it was hard to give up and fail. To this day, I have built meaningful relationships from this program, and I am thankful to have been a part of it. I graduated from college with a Bachelor of Science Degree in Health and Physical Education and a Master's in Human Service Counseling Health and Wellness. I am certified in Nutritional Therapy and I recently became Nationally Certified as a Health Education Specialist.

Achieving any of these accomplishments was no easy task, but I knew it had to be done.

No matter how much I accomplished, it wasn't enough to escape life's ups and downs. Shortly after moving back to New York, I got into a car accident which deemed me disabled for 10 agonizing months that forced me to dedicate most of my time in therapy. This moment in my life was made worse when I lost my job because of the lost time at work while I was in therapy. To me, being jobless and living back at home with my mom was like my worst fears coming to life! All this work to be independent and to be financially secure seemed to be for nothing. Again, here is this level of helplessness that I thought I was freed from that came back to haunt me.

Nevertheless, I had some very inspirational people that helped keep me encouraged and shortly after that I was able to rebuild what I lost and start my very own brand that focused on the two things I loved, Hair and Health! HairVentionZLLC was born. I also completed my masters online and took a mission trip to Rwanda, Africa! What a beautiful, emotional experience. One of which was on my bucket list that I achieved quicker than I thought. Once again, things were looking up. And I told myself God does not give you anything you can't handle. And no matter how many odds were against me, I was able to break the barriers. Have you ever experienced a loss after winning? How did you handle it?

Well, it would seem that my roller coaster ride was over, but of course, that's not how life works, right?! As a proud self-proclaimed planner, I always try to plan my life the exact way I want it, but of course, it doesn't always happen that way. In 2017, I moved to New Jersey for an opportunity to work in a salon which quickly fell through along with a failed relationship. In just 3 short months, my plan was flipped upside down. This unexpected turn of "unplanned" events put a tremendous strain on the goals I set for myself with this transition. I thought I was on my way to building and securing my future but look at me trying to plan my life once again. Some lessons take longer to learn than others, don't you agree?

Once again, I had to change course. Not only did I need to get on grind mode but also go back into survival mode. As you know this is something, I knew all too well growing up and having to do this again tore me apart. I felt like I was being faced with the hurt I tried to sweep under the rug all these years but left and right I was being tested. Every time I felt like I was winning in life, I always experienced a loss. I know many of you can relate. Often, I thought about suicide because I felt my whole life was nothing but pain. I have been searching and fighting to find the feeling of real happiness forever.

I had to start looking at myself. Was I the source of all the negativity and turmoil in my life? Even with the education and the determination, was my energy causing this tension in my life? I mean, I have visited a place that is most people's dream, and somehow, I would find the worst to say about it never focusing on the good I was able to experience. I felt that I could never focus on the good that came from my accomplishments because something would happen to remind me of the fear of not accomplishing enough, of not being good enough and settling with subpar potential. I often cried in my room, plenty times because I was just so fed up with constantly feeling bad about things that I could not control. I didn't want to share my pain with others because I felt that I would be viewed a certain way. I also did not want to burden anyone with my problems. I would hear the pride in my mom's words that I was the strong, independent one that she never had to worry about. I didn't want to let her down. I knew I had to change my mindset and believe again. So, I started to believe that as long as I stayed with my positive mindset, all things in my life will continue to flourish. I realized that most of the negative things that were happening in my life could have been caused by my negative thinking, so from that day forward, I vowed to stay optimistic and to speak life into my existence.

Developing a healthy mindset is tough, and it takes hard work, so you can just imagine how hard it was for me to develop and grow while struggling to overcome all of those unexpected changes. Many nights I prayed, asking God why are these things happening to me? What did I do to deserve such heartache? But who am I to question God? After all, my story is not my own. Maybe He was building me for something greater? Often in my prayers, I would ask God in what direction will my life go. He would give me ideas and tell me that one day, I would have to share my story.

I hope that my story not only inspires you but also lets you know that you are not alone in your struggles. Everyone handles situations differently, and as long as you can Break Those Barriers, you will always come out on top! Along the way in my journey, I came upon some healthy coping mechanisms that will help you in your journey to **Breaking Your Barriers.**

- Explore your hobbies and talents. I found what I was good at and focused on them. I discovered mine was hair, dance, reading, writing, and exercising. What talents, hobbies, or even passions do you enjoy? Seek them out and focus on them during your down time.

- Allow your passions to bring you joy. Instead of drowning in my past hurts, I started a business focused on one of my talents and passions, and it quickly became an outlet that relaxes me and allows me to help others which ultimately makes me happy. It's a gift, given to me by the Most High and one that He wants me to share with the world. Have you ever thought of becoming an entrepreneur? Having a small business or just selling items to friends and family? If so, get started, it can help you appreciate life more and find your purpose.

- Believe in happiness and then go for it! In order to be happy YOU have to create your own happiness, don't take life for granted, but try and live a life worth living doing the things you love. You will be unique and stand out because of it. Stay positive, post positive affirmations around your home or room, and watch your life change for the better.

Thanks to these tips today, I can proudly say that I am the CEO and founder of an on-demand Natural Hair Care and Wellness Company. I love my brand and what it stands for! Health, Beauty, and Hair Care, which are three of my most loved areas, and I get to pursue each one through my business. I am proud, not only, of the additional income my business brings, but I am also proud of how I was able to grow and become that much more of a master of my craft, just by owning my own business.

It was able to help me overcome the many setbacks; I experienced in my adulthood. I always had a passion for helping others, so creating my brand was an extension of my passions.

One of my favorite quotes from Pablo Picasso that I always remember when times get rough in life is *"The meaning of life is to find your gift. The purpose of life is to give it away."*

Once you have this embedded in your mind, you will live out your dreams. And remember to Break Those Barriers, don't let them break you!

About the Author

Ashley Crews was born and raised in Manhattan and Bronx, NY. She now resides in New Jersey, where she runs her own mobile hair care and wellness business (HairVentionZ) in which she not only styles natural hair but also educates her clients on maintaining a healthy lifestyle inside and out, while also working as a Public Health Educator for the

Department of Health. She holds a B.S. in Health and Physical Education and an M.A. in Human Services/Health and Wellness. She is also a Certified Health Education Specialist holding an additional certification in Nutritional Therapy. She has over 10 years of experience in the public health field, focusing on disease prevention and health promotion. Ashley has also written an eBook titled "Growing Natural: A Guide to Healthy Hair and a Healthier You. Her interest in wellness stemmed from her 6th-grade health education class, where she became interested in the human body and overall healthy practices. She is very excited that she had the opportunity to collaborate with such beautiful like-minded women to share her story and continue to lead women just like her to an everlasting healthy lifestyle.

"Hair is my passion; Health is my life."
- Ashley Crews founder of HairVentionZ

HairVentionZ: www.hairventionz.com
For inquiries email: ash@hairventionz.com
Connect with Ashley (Facebook and Instagram)
@HairventionZ

Power Booster #1
By Cathy Upshire

"It is a sad day when a woman loses her power,
because when you lose your power,
you lose yourself."

- Cathy Upshire, *"Woman Find Thyself"*

It is indeed a sad day when a woman loses her power, because power or the lack thereof, influences every area of our lives and the single most important thing a woman can do on her personal journey to wholeness, healing and authenticity is to take the necessary steps to RECLAIM it.

So, what is power? Power is the awesomeness you feel when you assume responsibility for your own happiness and overall sense of well-being. If you give that responsibility to anyone else, you might as well get out the Band-Aids, because you're going to need'em and *lots* of them.

So how do we give our power or personal responsibility away? If you're looking for someone else to make you happy, you're giving away your power. If you're looking for someone else to fix the broken parts of you, you're giving away your power. If you're looking for someone to make you feel good about yourself, you're giving away your power. If you're looking for someone to apologize before you can move on and forgive, you're giving your power away.

• • •

Power is responsibility, and the responsibility of maintaining a healthy sense of well-being is yours and yours alone. And I assure you if you don't take responsibility for these areas of your life, you're going to be in a corner somewhere licking your wounds; with no real sense of your true identity and wondering how the heck you got there.

Introspection

What have you given someone else the responsibility of doing for you in terms of *your* emotional well-being?

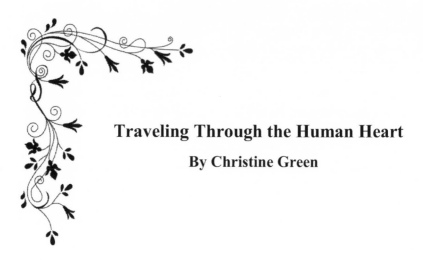

Traveling Through the Human Heart

By Christine Green

When you think of death, what is the first thing that comes to mind? You think of the loss of a loved one, right? And this is true, but death can also occur in other aspects of our lives as well. According to author Pat Convoy, the end of a marriage is the death of civilization. And when you are going through a divorce, it can certainly feel that way. When I was married to my first husband, I experienced endless heartache and pain. Not only did I endure mental and physical abuse, but I also suffered from his infidelity. In fact, he stepped outside our marriage many times, even before our first wedding anniversary. Can you imagine the pain and hurt I felt? I started to feel like I wasn't good enough or worthy of love. He was mentally cruel, as he often played mind games that affected my self-esteem and self-worth. He would make me feel guilty about things when, in fact, he should have been apologizing for the pain he inflicted on me. The days seemed endless as my tears flowed like a fountain from all the pain. Have you ever heard the phrase, "Things will get worse before they get better"? I didn't know exactly what that meant before this dark time in my life.

I do know that I was unhappy from the early stages in my marriage, but little did I know that it was only the tip of the iceberg! I remember telling my mother that our marriage wasn't going to last. Not only was he unfaithful, but he was also suffering from a drug addiction. His M.O. was to pick a fight so he could go on binges. No matter how good of a wife, I tried to be, I could not compete with the drugs. I remember waking up one morning telling myself, "This cannot be what God had in store for my marriage. There has to be better for me."

As I reflect on the past, I realize that this relationship was dying, and I was trying to perform CPR to save my marriage. But now I realize that I needed to allow things to run its course, even if it wasn't the course I chose. Emotionally, I was a wreck, and I did not realize how much it really had affected me. I felt bitter and hopeless. Can you imagine a bride feeling so abandoned? All I wanted was to love and to be loved. And like most women, even though the pain I was determined to put my best foot forward, so I kept pushing. One may ask why I stayed in the relationship for as long as I did. Why do most women stay? Family and finances.

The day I found out I was pregnant, I had mixed emotions. On the one hand, I was happy because I was going to have a child of my own, someone who would love me unconditionally. On the other hand, I was sad and scared because, in my heart of hearts, I knew my husband was not going to be the father he needed to be for our unborn child. And I was right. He was not there the majority of the pregnancy. As you can imagine, my pregnancy was very emotional. I went doctor's appointments alone. During this lonely time, my mom became my rock. She was there any time I called, and she took care of me as if I was a child again. In fact, she's the one who predicted I would have a son. Like most mother-daughter relationships, we didn't always agree, but one thing was for sure, and that is, she was going to be there for me through thick and thin. Remember when I said, "Things will get worse before they get better"? Well, things certainly got worse. As much as I know my mom wanted to be my super hero, she could not because of her life challenges. She was struggling financially and ultimately found herself without a home. It was a no brainer that I would open my and my husband's home up to her and my sister. It's not hard to imagine that my then-husband absolutely did not want them there. To be completely honest, it was pure hell. You could cut the tension in our house with a knife. Needless to say, my emotions were all over the place. He was making it impossible, and I felt like I had to choose between my family and my husband. I don't know about you, but I've learned that when faced with what feels like an impossible situation, I can only do one thing...PRAY! I cried many days during the course of the marriage. I prayed and asked God to direct my next step. I made it known that I didn't want to raise my son in chaos and unhappiness. My faith and love for my son have been my saving grace. When I received my answer from God, we all left and did not look back!

After this ordeal was over, I felt compelled to understand how I could even attract someone of such poor character. Reflecting on that relationship, it reminded me a lot of how my biological father treated me, my sister, and my mother. Just like in my first marriage, there were more bad times than good. He was selfish and a liar and growing up, it was his way or the highway. There were several occasions he was mentally abusive to my mother. He would go so far as writing her letters, tearing her down and being verbally abusive. I promised myself I would never date or marry a man who reminded me of my father. Growing up, we watched our mother struggle to take care of us. Even when the court ordered him to contribute financially, he refused. It's strange how history has a way of repeating itself when you don't resolve past pain. When I gave birth to my son (yes, my mom was right!), my ex-husband's behavior mirrored my father's. The biggest similarity is that neither my father or my son's father felt obligated to step up and take care of their responsibilities. Dealing with the inadequacies of my ex-husband brought up unresolved feelings of my childhood. I had so many mixed emotions from the things we suffered because my father refused to contribute to the care of his children. He made my childhood much harder than it had to be. Imagine coming home from school one day and when walking in the door, you learn that the electricity was turned off. For six months, we lived in our home with no electricity. Each day would we would have to rush home to complete our homework before the sun went down and it got dark. And when the school year was over, and summer came, as our poor luck would have it, this was one of the hottest summers our town had seen in many years. All I could think was, "What kind of father would allow his children to suffer like this?" Thank goodness one of our neighbors allowed us to stay in their home at night to keep cool. My mother and father went to court during this time, and I could not believe it when I heard with my ears as my father told the judge that he not only refused to pay but that he wanted us out the house! The judge asked, "Aren't those two girls your daughters?" When my father replied, "yes," the judge was so furious he had him removed from the courtroom. This was not the worse part. One day when my mother was gone, my father called a locksmith and had the locks changed and refused to give her a key! Nope, this was still not the worst part. I was in the home when the locks were being changed, and as much as I tried to stay in the home, my very own father pushed me out the door. He pushed me so hard that I fell on a bed of rocks and busted my mouth! Not only was I hurt, physically, and emotionally, but I was so angry. He did this to me when I was 10 years old! As I grew into an adult, I realized that I resented him for the many cruel things he did to the three of us. In fact, I carried this pain and anger with me until a good friend of mine told me, "you cannot heal what you do not address." For so long I thought I was past the things he had done, but to be honest, I was still holding on to it and was now attracting pain and hurt in my life through my relationships (remember that ex-husband I told you about?)

God did bring me the love of a father with my stepfather. He loved my sister and me as if we were his own children. Whenever I was having relationship problems, he would tell me what I needed to hear. The little girl in me appreciated the advice he gave from a father's point of view. As a young girl, I yearned for those father-daughter moments. With the love of the man, I would grow to refer to as my "father," I allowed myself to embrace those moments and fill the void that I once felt. This amazing man did everything a good father would do. Even though he came along in my adult life, he will always be my father. I loved his firmness and positivity. I allowed the little girl in me to smile and enjoy having a _Real_ father. Sadly, he passed in 2017, but I am forever thankful for our strong bond.

In 2018, my mother passed away, and I miss her so much every day. Before she died, she told me, "Baby, you have to forgive your father so that God can forgive you. I forgave him a long time ago". I've always admired and appreciated my mother's kind and forgiving spirit. Over time I've learned that you have to prepare yourself for an apology, you will never receive and prepare for a conversation you will never have. Eventually, I sent my father a message that simply said, "I forgive you." For the first time, I understood how people said that forgiveness is for you, not the other person. I felt a weight lift from my spirit, and I could finally let go of all the resentment I held in for so long.

In my healing, I realized that my father was the first man ever to hurt me, physically, mentally, and emotionally. As a mother, I never wanted my child to experience what I felt. More than anything, I wanted to set an example for my son by becoming the best version of myself. I knew that I could not do this alone. If it weren't for the love and support of other women, I don't know where I'd be. A major shift came when I decided to share my pain and vulnerability with my good girlfriend. Even when I wasn't quite ready, she lovingly helped me finally face the truth and make the needed adjustments in my life. But she wasn't the first to offer me sound advice. Even as a child, my spirit has always connected with women older than me, and I often felt God used them to reach me. Of course, my mother, even in her passing, was still a guiding force in my life. I find myself reflecting on our conversations when I was going through tough times. She and other elders offered the best advice on how to navigate the valleys of life. Each woman taught me something different. I wasn't always comfortable facing the things that bothered or scared me. But eventually, I learned that when you take the time to get comfortable with being uncomfortable with all aspects of your life, then you will learn a thing or two about yourself. I learned what I am capable of handling and how strong I truly am. Feeling scared, happy, excited, and a whole lot of other emotions are all a part of the process. I used to hide from my emotions, but you must understand that our emotions are a part of the journey. They are what mold us in certain situations. In my case, it was the unresolved emotions of resentment and anger that had taken over me.

Not only was I not open to forgiving my father, but I also wanted his pain and hurt to mirror my own. Yes! I wanted him to suffer! I wanted him to know what abandonment and betrayal felt like. When I was younger, I would talk to my mom when I was upset at my father. She would calm the storm stirring inside of me. But feeling this way did not sit well within in. It had gotten so bad I could barely face my own reflection in the mirror for months! Have you ever felt so much anger and resentment that you became unrecognizable to yourself? I knew it was time for me to face the truth because I was being consumed from the inside out.

It has been a long road to healing, but I can now say that the first step was the hardest! For me, it was acknowledging what my anger was doing to me and accepting that the only way I was going to find my way out of it was to forgive him. Self-reflection and self-evaluation opened my eyes to what the women in my life said to me. I was finally able to examine the root of the pain. It wasn't my ex-husband. He was just a reflection of the pain and anguish that was left from my first heartbreak with my father. I never thought I would get to this place, but eventually, I was able to send my father a message and let him know I forgave him. I remember thinking, "Even if he never responds to this message, you will know that you did your part and forgave him so that you can move on." It was like a cloud lifted from my heart, and again, the wise words of my mother came to me. A few years before she passed away, she told me that forgiveness is not for the other person it is for you. At the time, I didn't want to understand that concept. Like only a mother can, she kept is real with me. She told me that while I had an unforgiving attitude, he was still living life without a care in the world. You know, as I thought about what she said, I know I allowed these rotten feelings to occupy space in my mind and heart. The energy I put into being angry I could have used in a positive way.

As I continue to grow, I know how important it is to take a better approach to manage my emotions better. But forgiveness is not just for other people; it's something we must offer ourselves. We are human, and we are not always going to be cool and calm about everything. You're allowed to have your moments; the key is not to dwell on it. I encourage you to address what hurt you so that you can heal. If you let past pain fester without addressing it, then it will find a way to show up in other areas of your life. You will become the very thing you despise.

Are you ready to heal your heart, let go of the past and thrive? I am often asked how I broke free of the pain and anger I was carrying around for so long. This is what helped me, and I hope you too will take steps to be free and to thrive!

- Journal – Get one specific journal and keep it with you at all times so that you capture your thoughts and feelings so you can clear your mind and heart from all the negativity.
- Self-Development - Make and take time to do personal development so that you can be honest with yourself and so that you can pour healing into your life daily.
- Accountability - Seek wise counsel so that you can share your story, but also remains coachable and accept constructive feedback so you can heal.

Traveling through the human heart can be a challenge within, but if you go through it, you can get through it! In the end, it's well worth the travel! Forgiving my father has had a ripple effect on my life and my

● ● ●

relationships. I am happy to say that I am loving life! My fiancé and I are preparing for the arrival of our child and planning our wedding. I am learning to let go and let God. It is the best feeling in the world is to see your life reflect the love and kindness that is in your own heart.

About the Author

Christine Green is an author, speaker, licensed nurse, and certified health coach. Christine received a humanitarian award in 2018 for her service to her community. She also received the *Miz CEO, Entrepreneur on the Rise* award. Christine has been featured in the Huffington Post, Sheen Magazine and has graced the cover of the Courageous Woman Magazine. Christine helps her clients shape their lives around her favorite quote, *"Go confidently in the direction of your dreams. Live the life you've imagined."* ~Thoreau

Connect with Christine on Facebook @ChristineGreen and on Instagram @CoachAgryl
For inquiries email: NewNurse2011.CB@gmail.com

Power Booster #2
By Cathy Upshire

"Show me a woman who has given away her power, and I'll show you one who is somewhere licking her wounds."

- Cathy Upshire, *"Woman Find Thyself"*

I know this better than anyone because for many years my spirit was riddled with wounds that wouldn't heal; not because I didn't want them to, but because I didn't understand the connection between my lack of personal power and the state of my emotional wellbeing. I had given the responsibility for my happiness and well-being to anyone who came within inches of me and got disappointed every time. And for every disappointment, I encountered another wound was added to my already emotionally disfigured soul. And on any given day of the week (pick one) I was somewhere licking my wounds; trying desperately to soothe my aching heart.

But I was on a journey to reclaim my personal power and my lost identity; a journey to be whole. But what I discovered on my journey was that the closer I got to my destination, the less pain I felt. The more responsibility I took for my own . life and its outcomes, the less pain I was in. It was *considerably* less. I knew then I couldn't stop. And I vowed I'd never turn the responsibility of my happiness and well-being over to *anyone*. Happiness is an inside job. If you're looking for someone else to create it for you, you're committing emotional suicide by firing squad.

Reclaim Your Power. *Heal* Thyself.

● ● ●

<u>Introspection</u>

List some ways you've been disappointed by significant people in your life?   Were you expecting them to do something you were supposed to do for yourself or even something you weren't able to achieve yourself?

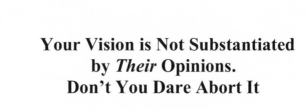

Your Vision is Not Substantiated by *Their* Opinions. Don't You Dare Abort It

By Dr. Cortesha Cowan

Some time ago, on a peaceful Sunday evening, I sat at my dining room table and browsed the internet and various social media sites from my laptop. After a short time of surfing, I came across a video of an engaging speaker – she honed in on the power of maintaining "vision." My mind and spirit were immediately taken to the initial birthing process of my organization, Mothers Helping Mothers Inc. [MHMI]. It started as a vision, that later manifested as a nationally renowned non-profit organization. I vividly recall writing out every little detail, the who(s), the what(s), the how(s), and the why(s). I wanted to effect change in my community and the world at large. Although, my [purposed] vision overwhelmed me, and my naysayers were/are innumerable; eventually, I understood my vision exceeded my personal apprehensions. I have long since learned that "vision" is

● ● ●

never about *us*, but always about Him and *them* [remember there are lives that only you will be able to compel change within].

Personally, the most significant realization at that moment was to understand the vision [my vision]. I knew *it* would come to pass… even if, I did not possess anything that was tangible or visible in front of me to ensure the manifestation. The uncertainties of my next move had nearly compelled me to give up. The naysayers, my lack of experience, my ignorance regarding entrepreneurship, my financial state, and the reality of who I was during that time [a 23-year-old mother of three, who I was also a teenage parent] … caused immobilizing self-doubt. We all know about *those* internal-talks… the mental battles we have regarding our God-given abilities. Although, our desires are directly linked to our purpose when it is time to "put the pedal to the metal," our logic produces apprehension; which makes "vision" obscured.

Consequently, the prerequisite task before negative thoughts settle *is* to seek God for clarity, instruction, provision, patience, and the wherewithal to see the vision through. I tell myself daily…that God is the same God of yesterday, today, and forever. Thus, He is always by my side. Irrefutably, I am a powerful woman of God, because what He placed within me is an unalterable reflection of Him. Please understand, *your* vision and *your* confidence are the most beneficial assets to possess. You may have been called or deemed a "so-called nobody," but God can supernaturally give you the revelation for [your] vision that will change everything in your life, *and* the lives of others.

For these reason(s), I encourage the teen mothers of Mothers Helping Mothers Inc. to embrace their vision and to understand that no one can take it from them [unless they allow people or things to deter them]. Typically, we don't realize how amazing and expansive vision is – it should exceed our abilities and expectations; if it doesn't, God's greatness will not be revealed! Prospectively, God will cause *your* purpose, passion, and plan to unfold [the "3P's" I utilize and educate others about vision] and navigate the implementation thereof within your life.

It is imperative to understand that God *gives* us the desires of our hearts; this translates to the fact that everything that is produced from us – is God's purpose(d) plan for us. What we desire to do, are the very things He created us to do - according to His will! Consequently, we will experience the wonder and accomplish great things in *His* name. God's purpose and plan for our lives nullify naysayers and provide the "yes" when reality said the answer should be "no!"

● ● ●

What is seen is not always the preface to an expected outcome. Don't let the appearance of failure or disaster stop *your* progression before you've started. You are a visionary. Therefore, you must understand the difficulties are inevitable, but God has anointed you for *this* vision, and the feeling of failure is just that… a feeling NOT fact! Learn from the difficulty, grow through the hardships, and utilize the experiences as fuel to keep striving. According to Hebrews 12: 1-2, Jesus is the author and the finisher of our faith… So, make it a practice to count it all joy, because you have already been declared the victor in every area of your life!

The supernatural power of vision is very real. However, it is imperative to do some essential things to ensure that you remain focused and unwavering! I encourage you to write your vision, make it plain, and establish a plan so you can see the manifestation. Additionally, those who support you will run with you, they will not minimize your vision, and they will not make you feel as if "your vision" is too much! Your God-sent supporters will provide relief, encouragement, and most importantly help!

Vision cannot materialize with a "self-seeking-me-myself-and I" mentality. Seek God and allow Him to guide you as you pursue your vision.

As you acknowledge God regarding your vision, He will constantly provide instructions and revisions of the vision! Remain attuned to the spirit, always consider the entire picture because you are a visionary, don't get distracted by the elements because they help illustrate the picture. Your vision wouldn't be God-ordained if it did not exceed your abilities, so embrace the struggle, because the vision will manifest beautifully.

Some may say embracing the struggle of seeing your vision materialize is easier said than done. Fortunately, God has provided a blueprint in His word. In order to gain access to your vision/destiny, self-assessment and fortitude are mandatory. II Corinthians 10: 3-5 states, "[3] For though we live in the world, we do not wage war as the world does.[4] The weapons we fight with are not the weapons of the world. On the contrary, they have divine power to demolish strongholds. [5] We demolish arguments and every pretension that sets itself up against the knowledge of God, and we take captive every thought to make it obedient to Christ." To put this scripture plainly, our vision can only manifest when we purposefully dismiss haters, pessimists, and even our thoughts of inadequacy and self-sabotage. We do this, by firmly asserting God's word over our lives with the understanding that what He has purposed will happen, regardless of what it looks like.

In Philippians 3:13, the Apostle Paul instructs us to forget about past failures and press forward into the manifestation of our vision! Thus, we must push through all the pain, every doubt, and focus on the vision. Visionary, I am speaking to you, God preestablished this for you. Trust me, I know how the middle feels…it is not easy! However, I have gained the control I need to facilitate the direction of my vision. Once we understand that our desires and goal are God-given… we can navigate the vision in a clear direction! Everything falls into place, and everything works out for our good! When I tapped into "The Source" [God]… I was granted more clarity to achieve the vision.

You must develop a clear plan for your life/vision; knowing your purpose will take you to the next level. Make every effort to strengthen your vision… remember it is from God. Once you have aligned your thoughts and actions with God and His word [completely], He will show you how to follow your vision and move beyond the people, their jealousy, and your apprehensions. Psalm 32:8 I will instruct you and teach you in the way you should go; I will counsel you with my loving eye on you.

So, when we encounter stumbling blocks while pursuing our vision, we mustn't misinterpret our victory because of our stumbles. God's orchestrated destiny within each one of us, and it is irrefutable. We cannot allow stumbling blocks to prevent us from fulfilling the vision God has given us.

I am living proof that tremendous blessings flow from our willingness to sow into another person's vision. We must all understand that our vision is directly connected to our willingness and ability to assist someone else. If we pay close attention to the vision that God has given us, then we should recognize that it has never been about how it will benefit our lives… but how it will advance God's people and God's plan. Your vision is the perfect establishment of God's love. Undoubtedly, I know that every person with a God-given goal, vision, or dream also possesses a personalized anointing to do what they are purposed to do. For this reason, without second-guessing ourselves, we can and will flourish within the vision God gave because it is His will!

Allow your vision to open *purpose-full* doors for you and slam the doors that serve as distractions and ungodly detours. As a visionary, surround yourself with people that strengthen and encourage you. Don't allow the pressure of the world to slow you down; you have a godly anointing that is coupled with supernatural vision, remain attuned… the favor on your life that is mind-blowing and God needs you to boldly walk in the supernatural anointing that dwells within you.

Your determination empowers your vision!

If you don't remember anything else, you've read… please remember my last words. For years, people did not understand what I was doing. They offered their unsolicited discouragement without considering their blatant negativity. They often uttered things like, "Girl *this* [my vision] is a lot… how are you doing it without money?" I never responded to *their* perspective… but I gave my focus to my faith. Then I responded, "Just because *you* haven't seen it, it does not mean it isn't there."

I pursued and regained my prosperity. That made this mission great and unforgettable! My beginnings keep me humble and eternally grateful; because I know God brings us through uncertainty – so He can take us to the place He has prepared for us. I examine my accomplishments, and I recall every teenage mother and the women I have been able to help daily. When we remain focused on the vision, our minds become trained to only consider the Word of God as our point of security; and in turn, the vision cannot appear or obscured by anything! Nothing else matters when God gives His stamp of approval! I am telling you now, God has prophetically authored your life and sealed it with His guarantee!

The word of God states in Luke 22:32, "but I have prayed [especially] for you, that your faith [and confidence in Me] will not fail; this scripture exemplifies God's unwavering commitment to us and His will. God won't allow us to fail, because that means *He* fails, and we know it is impossible for God to fail – II Corinthians 12:9 declares, "And He said unto me, My grace is sufficient for thee: for my strength is made perfect in weakness. Most gladly, therefore, will I rather glory in my difficulties, that the power of Christ may rest upon me." Thus, we can rest assured that our success in Him is certain; because our vision is *purposed,* and our purpose requires *vision,* God thoroughly equips us to what others deem impossible. Simply because, God cannot reveal His glory without the presence of naysayers, mountains, valleys, trials, and hardships.

Here's the simple formula for you to follow that will allow you to blissfully watch the vision emerge right before your eyes:

- Establish an unbreakable grip on your vision
- Make the plan
- Keep the faith and
- Do the work

Our successes have never been in the hands of man or determined by the words of a man or woman; "Human beings cannot live on bread alone, but we live [and succeed] by every word that God speaks" [Matthew 4:4]. I encourage you to give NO credence to the opinions of "them," but firmly grasp God's promises, speak them, believe them, and never forget them. God has made plans for you; those plans are good and perfect for you. He will not hurt you. God's plans provide hope and a prosperous future [Jeremiah 29:11]. Therefore, dismiss the negative thoughts and cynics, go back to the plans, the dreams, and most importantly take hold of the vision God has given you! Your time has come, and you will not surrender to the difficulty. God has called you by name, and he knows who you are! You are one of His visionaries – don't you dare abort the vision!

About the Author

Dr. Cortesha Cowan, author, speaker, and founder/CEO of Mothers Helping Mothers (MHM) Inc., was a teen mom who grew up in Lima, Ohio. With the support of her family and her innate drive to succeed, Dr. Cowan maintained school attendance, activities, and employment until graduation. Dr. Cowan is a childcare teacher and is the founder/CEO of Cozy Corner Home of Care & Love, a childcare center located in Columbus, Ohio.

"Dr. Cowan is known as "The Confidence Coach" for her ability to help women and young girls grow their confidence and passion for what they are trying to do. She is a straightforward coach with a passion for helping women and young girls.

As a female-entrepreneur, she has worked hard to build a step-by-step system and amazing model for opening homes for teen and young mothers that are homeless and in need of support services. She has leveraged her professional and personal experience to empower and help teen mothers, young girls, and women grow. Dr. Cowan's life's mission is to educate, empower, and support others. In 2008, God gave Dr. Cowan the vision to help teen mothers to become self-sufficient by being a resource to young mothers and their children. This vision expanded to providing safe shelter at the Haven of Hope crisis and transitional house and empowerment through programs at MHM and local partner organizations. In addition to receiving an Honorary Doctorate Degree, Dr. Cowan is also a certified life coach. Dr. Cowan has received numerous awards for her commitment to helping others, including the International Women's Day recognition award.

To learn more about Dr. Cowan visit
www.DrCorteshaCowan.com
For inquiries email Dr. Cowan at
DrCorteshaCowan@gmail.com
Connect with Dr. Cowan on social media
@DrCorteshaCowan

Power Booster #3
By Cathy Upshire

"Setting boundaries isn't enough. We must have the courage to impose consequences when those boundaries are being violated or ignored."

- Cathy Upshire, *"Woman Find Thyself"*

I was watching the Dr. Phil show one afternoon. He was talking to a guest about the importance of setting boundaries. But he went on to say; boundaries weren't enough. He said if they're not coupled with consequences, the behavior will persist. And here's what I know for sure...he's right!

One of the greatest pieces of advice I was given as a young woman was given to me by my cousin, friend, and confidante, Joyce Tucker. She said, "Cathy when you change, the people around you will change." It was the best advice I'd ever received, but it was the advice it took the longest to execute. I just couldn't comprehend something so simple could be so true. But 15 years after I received her advice, I learned it *was* true. Any change I saw in *anyone* as it related to me on my journey started with me mustering up the *courage* to ruffle a few feathers when the boundaries I'd set for myself were crossed; sending a *clear* message that their behavior towards me was NOT acceptable. I was willing to fight for my dignity—what little bit of it I still had left—and if it meant rocking the boat or tipping it over, I was prepared to go down with the ship.

You cannot enforce a boundary by "keeping the peace." As Dr. Phil McGraw said, *"If there are no consequences, the behavior will persist."* And Depak Chopra, a two times New

York bestselling author, *"Every great change is preceded by chaos."* Change starts with YOU.

Introspection

Name a boundary you've set for yourself? Has that boundary been violated by a significant person in your life? What were the consequences of that violation? Did you confront them; did you let it go? Are they even aware a boundary has been crossed?

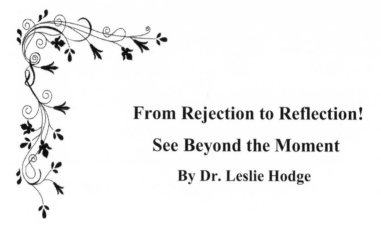

From Rejection to Reflection!
See Beyond the Moment
By Dr. Leslie Hodge

It was all a dream; I used to read…wait, wait, wait, let me stop. There I go again having a *"good Christian girl who loves trap music"* moment. You know those moments, when one minute your mind and spirit are in a state of praise and worship, and before you know it, a desire or some would say, a need, come over you, and you need to hear some "trap music" with a banging beat…sometimes with the parent advisory warning version, and at other times the radio or Walmart version will be due. I know my heart, mind, and soul must be conflicted, because I am going from one extreme to the other, and often at a slow, steady pace. However, at other times it is a quick, no time for a warning, a shock to the system. You know, just like life!

In life we do not always get to brace ourselves for rejection – the letdown, the left out, the looked over, the change in heart, the change of mind, the passed by or the moments we are forgotten. Sometimes those moments of rejection appear in our lives just like our music playlists on shuffle mode…one minute you're listening to *For Your Glory by Tasha Cobbs Leonard* and the next song that plays is *DNA by Kendrick Lamar.*

I am Dr. Leslie Hodge, and I know rejection. Yes, I have experienced rejection from family, friends, strangers, work, church, online, and in every other area of my life. For the politically correct, I have experienced familial, social, occupational, spiritual, environmental, and physical rejection. I've learned over my 4 decades of life that you must call a thing a thing. Rejection is rejection. Rejection hurts. Rejection cuts. Rejection is not fun. Rejection not only hurts emotionally but physically and mentally too. Studies show that our brains process rejection the same way it processes pain after being hit in the stomach. Ouch! To be transparent, when I have experienced rejection in my life, it caused devastation, humiliation, intimidation, and isolation.

As I reflect on my life, I cannot specifically pinpoint when I first experienced rejection, but I can tell you that it was at a young age. Whether the rejection is intentional or not, the result of choices made by others or someone exercising their preferences in my life, it is still a rejection. Being the last one selected for the kickball team, not receiving an invitation to the birthday party or sleepover, not being asked to the school dance, not being picked for the part in the school play, not being accepted into the university or college of choice, not being hired for the job, not being selected for the "special team" on the "special project" at work, not being granted the promotion, not being selected as the lead soloist of the choir, not receiving the marriage proposal, not getting the contract, not being asked to join co-workers for lunch, not being invited on the girls' trip or family vacation, not having your posts liked or shared on social media, not having your friends and family support your business, buy your book or attend your events, or not being included in the email thread, not...not...not. All of these "not" moments have one thing in common – they can all create a feeling of rejection.

The interesting thing about rejection is that it does not always come in a direct or clear-cut *NO*. At times, it can come in the forms of "not this time," "You interviewed well, but...", "I wish we could, but...", "I think it's best if we just remain...", the all too familiar, "Oops, I thought I sent...!" or just plain silence. It does not matter the verbiage used or if there is no response (silence), the result is the same...you feel rejected, and it hurts.

Pause and take a few minutes to ask yourself one question, "When I am rejected, does that mean my feelings are hurt?" For me, I can respond with a resounding, YES! Yes, my feelings are hurt, were hurt, and probably would remain hurt if I had not begun developing a proper response to the thoughts and feelings that accompany the "R" word – *rejection.*

Life is filled with making decision after decision after decision. The reality is, not making a decision, is making a decision. How you choose to process rejection is a decision. How you choose to react to rejection is a decision. Your response to rejection is a decision. Let's face it; rejection is a part of living. It is a part of life. Everyone is not going to like you, invite you, book you, support you, vote for you, or include you...for various reasons, but their decision should not change how you view yourself. Although it has taken me decades to come to a decision on how I will deal with rejection, one thing I now understand, is after you have experienced enough rejection, and taken enough rides on the mental and emotional roller coaster of rejection, you discover that the ups and downs, highs and lows, self-sabotaging, and the behaviors of over-exaggeration, are based on the ideas and preferences of someone else.

I used to dislike (only because hate is such a strong word) playing games that require a selection process. When I tell you, it triggered something in me, it did. Now, don't get me wrong, I didn't have to be like the NFL's #1 draft pick on draft day, but at the same time I did not want to be like the last draft pick either, who is referred to as "Mr. Irrelevant" (for all of the non-NFL fans who read this, this is really how the last pick is announced). I truly disliked wondering if I was going to be selected near the beginning or be the last (wo)man standing. In the event I was selected near the end or flat-out last, I found myself going into the *"I'm going to show them"* or the "I must prove to "them" and show "them" what they missed out on" mode. But with maturity and growth, I had to pause and ask myself, "Why?". Why did I need to "show them?" Why did I feel the need to "prove" myself? Why did I care about how others viewed me?

As I said before, rejection can happen in any area of life. For me, some of the most life-changing moments of rejection happened at work. A few years ago, I was filled with the desire to do something different, to challenge myself, and to take on new responsibilities. I decided to apply for a newly created position within my company, whose job responsibilities included 40% of what I loved to do – training and teaching my colleagues and their supportive staff. The job description was perfect. I was encouraged to apply and even met with a colleague who already held the position in another state. She helped me prepare for both rounds of interviews. After successfully completing the first round, the applicant pool was down to 3 people. After the second round of interviews, the applicant pool was now down to 2 people – another candidate and me. I remember it like yesterday. I was at work preparing to give evaluations to my staff when suddenly I had an incoming call from my supervisor. After we exchanged pleasantries, she said the famous words, "You interviewed well, but we've decided to go with the other candidate." Although it was communicated in a pleasant, professional, and considerate manner, the result was the same – rejection.

Rejection is a double-edged sword. It causes revelation and confirmation. What you think about yourself, rejection reveals it. What you think you deserve, rejection reveals it. What you think you can become, rejection reveals it. And just as rejection reveals what you think about yourself, what you think you deserve, and what you think you can become, it also confirms what you think about yourself, what you think you deserve and what you know you were created to be.

There's a saying that the older you get, the wiser you become. Well, let's just say that I have become wiser, especially when it comes to rejection. After yet another, "You interviewed well, but we've decided to go with the other candidate" moment, you talk about a blow to the ego, I had a mentor tell me it was ok to cry, it was even ok to be mad, but it was not ok to doubt my abilities or not focus on what I had learned. While heeding to her advice, I discovered the importance of reflection.

Reflection after rejection changes your perception. Whoa, I think I just said something. If I were a pastor, and this was my sermon, the congregation would say, "Preach Pastor!". Reflection after rejection can literally save you from yourself – the mental and emotional anguish and exhaustion of thinking of countless ways to get revenge on the ones who rejected you, or you trying to prove that their decision about you was incorrect. Choosing reflection after a rejection is not for the other party; it is for you!

Reflection can bring clarity and change. Instead of asking "Why me?", and wallowing in sadness, pity and shame, reflection can cause you to ask, "Why not me?". Rejection is not a personal malicious attack against you. Yes, it happens to you, but it is never about you in the present moment. It is about you developing to ensure you become who you were designed to be. I like to think of moments of rejection experienced throughout life, are similar to cement trucks pouring the foundation for a new house or building. The cement is poured to create a solid foundation for the construction of a new house or building. If the foundation is not strong, then the structure is subject to fall with any whisper of wind or storm. Doesn't that sound like life? Whether rejection is the result of a breakup, job loss or end of a friendship, once you realize rejection is part of the foundation needed for you to grow and develop, then you will not allow the whispers you replay over and over in your mind and the storms you have to walk through in life, to destroy you. Choosing to take time to reflect on the whispers and storms in life help you see beyond the moment. Life is filled with ups and downs, tosses and turns, but when you stop and look at the big picture, you will see that rejection was necessary. All the moments of rejections were necessary for your protection, as you prepare for one thing – your destiny.

Why not me? That is a question we seldom ask ourselves. The answer is rejection is protection from settling. Think back, had you gotten the promotion, then you would have never started your business. Had you received the proposal, then you would be married to him, instead of the man designed just for you. Had you received the support, then you would remain in your comfort zone, instead of interacting and gaining the support of strangers turned supporters. See, rejection is all a setup. A setup for you to reflect on where you are, where you are going, and where you are supposed to be. Reflection from rejection helps you see beyond the moment. The moment is just a piece of the big picture. It's those moments that will push us to the mountain top. And let me tell you, the view from the top is a whole lot better.

It is time to up your mind game. If you're going to shift from hoping to being…wallowing to living…surviving to thriving, then you must **S.T.O.P.** –

Start believing the **T**ruth about yourself despite **O**ther's **P**erceptions

Is that a mouth full? Yes, but more importantly, it's a life-changer. Since you've decided to live a Thrive Girl Thrive Life, then you can no longer remain in your comfort zone, or settle into thoughts and ideas about yourself, based on someone else's perception of you. Change your mind, change your life.

By no means do I have this journey called life figured out, but when I decided to S.T.O.P., and believe what God says about me, life changed. Because He says, I am the head and not the tail. I believe it is true for my life. Because He says, I am above and not beneath. I believe it is true for my life. Because He says, I am the lender and not the borrower. I believe it is true for my life. Because He says, victory is mine. I believe it is true for my life. Because He says, all things work together for my good. I believe it is true for my life. Because He says, I am fearfully and wonderfully made. I believe it is true for my life. Because He says, He has plans for me. I believe it is true for my life. Because He says that He is my friend. I believe it is true for my life. Because He says, no weapon formed against me will prosper. I believe it is true for my life. Therefore, since He says it, and I believe it, that settles it. Anything that is done or said that contradicts what He says, I have to **S.T.O.P.!**

You may not realize it, but your reaction to rejection is a reflection of what you believe to be true about yourself. Not receiving the promotion doesn't mean you are a poor employee. But, if you believe that, then you stop doing your work or start missing deadlines, instead of taking advantage of the opportunity to identify areas that need improvement, so you are an even better candidate for the next promotion.

Not being asked for your hand in marriage does not mean you are not worthy of being someone's wife. But, if you believe that, then you begin dating and engaging in activities irresponsibly, instead of learning more about yourself and defining what you like and dislike, while trusting and believing that greater is in store for you.

It's a new day, which means it is a new opportunity to think differently and set new expectations and standards for yourself. The time has run out for others to label and define you by their standards. You have outgrown the box they want to keep you in. The box is now in the trash compactor, never to be used again. The self-imposed limits that you have placed on your mind and abilities have been snatched off like a bandage covering a wound. Just like yesterday's news, let their perceptions of you be a thing of the past. Begin seeing yourself through the lens of boldness, power, and strength. Begin seeing yourself shift from good to great...from the balcony to the front, row...from the opening act to the main attraction. Begin seeing yourself...see beyond the moment and most importantly remember to **S.T.O.P.**

About the Author

As a pharmacist, entrepreneur, speaker, author, radio host, certified coach, and magazine contributor, Dr. Leslie Hodge creatively pairs her passion for people with her commitment to serving others. Dr. Hodge selflessly equips, enhances, and empowers people from all walks of life.

Dr. Hodge was reared in a Christian household that promoted education and service. Throughout her life, she remained mindful of the biblical passage:" I can do all things through Christ that strengthens me." Dr. Hodge earned her Doctor of Pharmacy Degree (PharmD) from Purdue University. She also holds the American Pharmacists Association (APhA) certifications in Pharmacy-Based Immunization Delivery and Delivering Medication Therapy Management Services.

Operating in her commitment to service and being a resource for patients and families to manage their medications better and improve their health, Dr. Hodge founded *Scripts & Beyond – A Pharmacist Focused On YOU*™. Scripts & Beyond is a medication review and consulting company which specializes in providing one-on-

one medication therapy management services. She is also the founder of *Reflections Coaching & Consulting – Let the True YOU Emerge*™. She helps high-achieving men and women create balance and wellness in the 7 areas of life (spiritual, financial, physical, intellectual, occupational, emotional, and social).

Dr. Hodge can be found dispensing a dose of health, wellness, and lifestyle tips, as a featured speaker and a contributing writer for print and online magazines.

Scripts & Beyond, LLC - **A Pharmacist Focused On YOU™**

Reflections Coaching & Consulting, LLC - **Let the True YOU Emerge™**

www.drlesliehodge.com

For inquiries email: info@drlesliehodge.com or call 888-415-0656

Connect with Dr. Hodge (Facebook and Instagram) @drlesliehodge or on LinkedIn linkedin.com/in/leslie-hodge

Power Booster #4
By Cathy Upshire

"People aren't necessarily causing your pain. Not getting what you think you need from them is. Become whole, and you will find what you thought you needed you won't need anymore."

- Cathy Upshire, *"Woman Find Thyself"*

When I began my journey to wholeness, I was a hot mess. I had several things I needed from select individuals; namely their acceptance and approval. But I aspired to be whole, and it was all I could think about for an entire year. I thought about what it would mean to be happy; to be free of my emotional pain. I thought about the things that made me hurt inside; then ask myself why I found them so hurtful. I thought about those who didn't accept me and why it panged me so much; why those, why them, why not her or him. I thought about those who hurt me. Did they do something, or did I want something they weren't willing to give? I started questioned *everything*. I sought out ways to take control of my life; my emotional well-being; myself. I became self-centered but in a good way. When I felt scared, I stopped to ask myself, what are you afraid of? For the mistakes I made, I asked what I could've done differently. I told myself the unadulterated truth about everything. I was determined to crack the code to unlock the prison doors that kept me emotionally bound for so long.

Fast forward:
I was WHOLE again. And everything had changed. The people who seemed so tall; even larger than life seemed so insignificant, minuscule and small. The acceptance and

approval I so desperately needed of them all but disappeared. I went from *wanting* to be in their lives to not wanting them in mine because they had not proven themselves worthy. Everything I thought I needed, miraculously, I didn't need anymore. I was whole. It was then I realized people had very little to do with my emotional pain and that my *lack* of Personal Power was the culprit.

Introspection

How have you been hurt by significant people in your life? What exactly did they do; was it something they *did* to you or something they didn't *give* you?

Balance...Keeping it Together
and Finding Your Rhythm as a Mother
By Dr. Lisa Greene Henderson

Mommy, ma, mama, mom…. however, the variation
of the word is used; this is the one role that can challenge
and humble even the most equipped or educated woman to
her core. As a little girl, I dreamed, as many girls do, of
becoming a mother. It was on my checklist of things to
accomplish – graduate from High School – check; go to
college – check; get a masters – check; graduate from school
with a doctorate – check; marry a good Christian guy with a
job who has good family values – check; get a job in the field
I actually went to school for – check, and then have children.
And of course, all this was to be done before I turned 30! I
know…just a little type "A" or some would call it being
"driven." I won't lie, God has blessed me with a loving
family, in-laws that I actually like and love, great
friendships, and of course God is at the center. Yes, there

were and continue to be challenges along the way, growing pains, but no major setbacks in my life…life is and has been good. But even with the sunshine that warmed my life sometimes, I found myself looking at the lives of others and wondered if it could be better. Over the years I had to learn to apply the old adage of "the grass isn't always greener on the other side" and remember that the grass is just as green on my side as it is on someone else's side. For me to not be envious or covet the lives of others, there were two rules of thought I kept close. First, I would remind myself that you never know what crap may be going on in someone else's life that is making their grass so green. Second, I knew that we all have different paths in life and that there is enough success for each of us. More than anything, I knew that I had to embrace and love the life I had because it is my life, and it is good. My attitude directly impacts how I view my life – positively or negatively. On paper, each of us sounds darn good, but this doesn't mean a thing if our hearts and attitudes aren't right – and we must be honest with ourselves about this. So, how does this tie into the role of being a mom…well for me it has been and continues to be the most humbling, frustrating, and challenging role I've experienced and continue to experience. If you're a mom, then you've likely come to realize that this most esteemed role is fluid and you must be able and willing to adjust and adapt if you want to see the fruits of your belly to prosper.

I remember having accomplished my checklist by 30. Yes, at 30, I was with child and overjoyed to embark on my life dream of becoming a mother. You can image the devastation when we were told it wasn't a viable pregnancy, and I ended up having a miscarriage. Before learning that this was a common occurrence for many women, I went through my own mental torture, asking myself so many questions. Why did this happen? Did I do something wrong? Am I not capable of having a child? All of the self-defeating thoughts you could have, I had them and then some. The hit to my self-esteem was hard, and I wallowed in this state for a while. For me, giving life was a part of my role as a woman. And, as I mentioned earlier, you can "have it all," but this one thing can take you out. Time healed the emotional wound and loss. I adopted the mindset of my body wasn't ready to be a vessel to carry a child and had to get itself ready. So, here we go again…another pregnancy, but this one was not without emotional angst. We got through the first trimester… whew, no miscarriage, we should be good. Ha! Not the case, test results suggested possible genetic issues which then turned into each subsequent doctor's visit starting with the disclaimer "you know you can still terminate the pregnancy." All I could think was, "I can't terminate this pregnancy. I'm a Christian!" The unknown gave way to the mental and spiritual battle that ensued in my head...and questioning if I had the emotional bandwidth for this. It was not fun, but it was my journey, and I often felt that no one understood despite their expressed concern. How humbling for me, a person who liked control was completely out of control. And, as most of us do when things feel out of control, I sought some type of control; which was for me getting additional ultra sounds to monitor the baby, researching, and peppering the doctor with my many questions. In my mind, I was doing something. Then finally out of the woods and yet another thing to test my faith came up, at a routine visit. I was sent to the hospital for observations – I had developed pre-eclampsia. In simple terms, this means my body was rejecting the baby. Really?!?! This motherhood thing had already taken a lot of me, now this, and the baby wasn't even here yet! So, at 33 weeks into the pregnancy a day of observation turned into a week stay, a high risk labeled pregnancy and meetings with high-risk obstetricians and neonatal intensive care unit (NICU) doctors. Here is where ignorance is bliss but not for me, thanks to my education and Mr. Google, who told me everything I needed to know about the potential risks. The possible developmental delays that would come with a premature birth or even the realization that one of us might not make it through this situation were adding to my stress. This, for me, was the most humbling time at this point in my life — total surrender. I had so many medications being pumped into me to give the little life in me a fighting chance. I laid on the hospital bed, looking like a beached whale, remembering the flow of friends and family coming through. Aware that life still goes on, I found the humor in the small moments…like one of my girlfriends deliberating over who she was going to vote to be The Next American Idol and then finally getting on her phone to cast her vote for Fantasia to be the winner. After all of the daytime traffic, I was often left alone in the quiet of the night with only the beeps from the machines connected to me. Talk about vulnerable, scared, and the unknown!

With the speeding of the baby's lung development came the induced pregnancy. Of course, I really had no control over my body or even the outcome of what was to come, but I do remember the way my girls did their part to help bring our tiny little life into the world. As my hubby's booming voice filled the room, they knew exactly how to manage him and me during this time. After delivery, the drama of our pregnancy continued to play out, and we were definitely not out of the woods. While the medical team worked on me, the pediatric team whisked the baby off to the NICU for what would turn out to be a week-long stay. When we were finally released from the hospital, my debut into motherhood was still not free and clear. We received the wonderful parting gift of an infant heart monitor that the baby was required to wear for the next couple of months. OMG! Whenever the monitor would make the smallest beep, it would freak the living daylights out of us! Is he breathing? Shake him a little! Are those darn leads attached? But at the end of the day, there was a victory! A life! A miracle! Plus, the emotional and spiritual growth that came with it. Even now, when I look at my body and can see the belly fat that remains, it is a constant reminder that what I went through was all worth it!

Even with the drama of the first delivery, I was crazy enough to try this pregnancy thing again. Thankfully God spared me the second time around with a pretty non-eventful pregnancy. When you compare the two, it was like night and day. The second was full-term, he was breached at one point but quickly figured out how to turn himself in the right direction. I had dilated overnight from 3cm to 9cm, was rushed to the hospital, no time for drugs, but given a warm compress – really?? Then the world welcomed my healthy second born, and instead of the post-delivery drama, I was given a menu and asked what I wanted to have for lunch. God definitely has a sense of humor!

Each of us has our own story of pregnancy and childbirth. We are impacted by this "women's work" even if we are simply on the journey with a friend going through a pregnancy, or even if we adopt a baby. Regardless of the situation, becoming a mother is no joke! But then the realization hits home that this is only a small fraction of that child's life and your journey with them is just beginning. The child still has to grow up and guess what… you are a key player in this. Yep, ready or not as a mother you are tasked with the challenge to love – more specifically love unconditionally, invest, forgive, let go, take back, celebrate, sacrifice, laugh, cry, teach, train, and even give that tough love. We may never feel equipped as mothers. But for me, as a Christian, being grounded in the scriptures helps gives me a foundation to work from. The scriptures remind me that in my weakness I am made strong; that God will not give you more than you can handle or bear; and I can do all things through Him who give me strength. These and so many more scriptures form my foundation and allow me to draw strength. For each of you, it maybe this same source or another, but you each need a foundation to draw strength from.

The journey of being a mother, whether alone or with a partner, is a personal journey. For as your child grows, you too have no choice but to grow and evolve to be effective, relevant, and impactful. I remember in my doctoral program, a class on object relations and learning about Donald Winnicott's concept of "good enough mothering." To paraphrase, it is where the mother starts out totally devoted to her newborn, from not getting any sleep, at the baby's beck and call; sacrificing her own needs to helping the baby experience some independence gradually. A mother instinctively understands not readily meeting every need is a part of healthy development and cognitive growth. This part is not always easy for most of us who want to earn our "good mother" badge. But being a good mother means adapting, or better put "constantly adapting" for your children and for yourself. Simply put, as a mother, to be your best, you must step back and take care of yourself. It is not selfish by being aware of what you need to be effective and whole as a woman, so in turn, you can be a good mother.

Let's be honest if you are not healthy emotionally, physically, and spiritually you can't meet your own needs, let alone your child's needs. As a mother, you set the tone of your household. Are you stressed? Moody? Disorganized? Or are you upbeat? Faithful? Positive? These are just a couple of things that can affect your child's emotional and physical development and their responses to you. Remember you don't have to be perfect, but you have to be good enough and put forth an effort. If you don't invest in you, then you won't get the returns on motherhood that you desire and hoped for. Instead, you will be frustrated, resentful, and scared. Sound familiar?

The first step in understanding what contributes to your mothering style is to reflect on how you were parented. Your parents set that first impression, that template you either vow to never be like or vow to never do to your child what your parents did to you. Then one day we all have that epiphany... "I am turning into my mother." You realize that what was said to you growing up was actually right and full of wisdom, and you are trying to incorporate those same values and lessons in rearing your child. Raising a child in today's society is different from how you or I were raised. The influence of social media is ever-present, and boundaries are constantly being tested. This makes it even more important for us as mothers to be aware of what we are dealing with, not ignoring, or dis- equipping our child. Our children are a reflection of us - the good, the bad, and the ugly. Each developmental phase of your child's life requires you as a mother to be prepared – do the research, stay current, be involved, ask the questions, and make your child feel valued. Children need to have clear boundaries, know the rules, have structure, and above all know that they are loved. Again, for these things to be effective, as a mother, you need to have them in check. Don't expect your child to do something that you are not willing to try or do. Your child is always watching and take their cues from you. If you have multiple children remember that each child is different - take the time to get to know each, not compare them, or gravitate to the easier child. Raise your children. Don't have them raise each other, their friends raise them, or social media raise them. Yes, you are busy. Yes, you want to have fun and relax. Yes, they may be getting on your nerves. But they also bring you great joy. Remember the journey it took to bring them into the world.

The goal as women, especially as mothers is to thrive and not just survive. Quality of life is important. As Stephen Covey states in "The 7 Habits of Highly Effective People" - be proactive, not reactive and to begin with the end in mind. What is your end goal as a woman, a mother? Put this in action and get the support you need - family, friends, and other resources. Have those couple of people in your life that you trust who can tell you the truth in love and you not get an attitude. Work at not letting your fear consume and paralyze you. Be open to seeking professional help. As a clinical psychologist, too often, the children I treat in therapy have some issue with their mother. Let's not continue to be a part of the problem, but a part of the solution by getting ourselves the help we need to thrive, be mindful/self-aware, and balanced.

Being a mother is a process. Celebrate the victories and keep your joy in the tough times. Be willing to go through the process. Don't stop being your best because you aren't where you think you should be. Be willing to re-evaluate regularly your approach as a mother. Don't just do something because you have always done it that way. Ask yourself – why am I doing what I am doing? See what is working, what is not, and change as a woman and mother. Get help to change if you can't do it by yourself. Don't live in the negativity of your mistakes as a mother because there will be many. Remember, you want to be your best self, which in turn will lead to you being the best mother you can so that when you look back on your journey you will be pleased.

I end with this, being a mother is a life long journey. Right now, I am in the adolescent and teenage phases with my two boys, they are healthy, doing well academically, socially, and growing spiritually. I love them to death, but they stretch me out especially with their attitudes because in these developmental phases they are constantly testing of boundaries, trying to figure out their identity, and are wrestling with staying connected and individuating. I get it wrong with them, I tell them I am sorry, and I tell them when they have hurt my feelings. My clinical skills are like kryptonite to them. They have seen me frustrated, cry, advocate for them, hurt when they hurt, and celebrate their victories. At times I am told "you are doing too much," but they know I love them as I tell them this often. I work hard to be the best example of love and character for them. I am not perfect, but I try. My challenge to each of you is just simply to try.

About the Author

Dr. Lisa Greene Henderson holds both a Doctorate in Clinical Psychology and a Master's degree in Community Counseling from the George Washington University in Washington, DC. She is licensed in the State of Maryland, the District of Columbia, Virginia, and is a Registered Psychologist in her home country of Bermuda.

Dr. Henderson has more than 18 years of experience in the field and has worked in several settings, including the school system; university counseling centers; psychiatric hospitals; prison system/court services; medical centers; and office-based and home-based private practices. Dr. Henderson has worked with all ages providing individual and group therapy. Dr. Henderson has been invited over the years to speak at various organizations on topics including parenting, child development, depression in women, and domestic violence.

Dr. Henderson is an active member of the American Psychological Association, Delta Sigma Theta Sorority, Incorporated, and the Prince George's County Chapter of Jack and Jill of America, Incorporated. Dr. Henderson is married to prominent international businessman formerly of the World Bank and the United States Commercial Service/Commerce Department Eric Henderson. She is the mother of two sons, William 15 and Jackson 13.

Power Booster #5
By Cathy Upshire

"Holding a grudge will strip you of your power far quicker than any person will.

- Cathy Upshire, *"Woman Find Thyself"*

You've heard it, "No one can take your power away, you give it away." The first time I heard those words, a lightbulb went off in my head, and I thought about the many ways I was giving away mine. And, surprisingly, the one that topped the charts, hands down, was the inability to let go of past hurts and offenses and forgive.

One might say, "What does that have to do with power?" Everything. Fact is...holding on to past offenses and grudges will strip you of your power far quicker than any person will. And here's the clincher...the person for whom you're carrying that grudge is the very person you're giving your power to, and they can impact your sense of well-being without much effort at all.

Not only that—but you can give away our power without anyone even being on the receiving end. I went to someone once about an offensive comment they made after holding on to a year-long grudge. I told them what they said and how offended I was and a few other things. They were stunned! It turns out...they genuinely had no idea the comment was offensive and thanked me for educating them on it.

The moral of this story? I didn't give *them* my power; I gave it to dead space. What a tragedy. A whole year of negative energy in my body, countless hours of that person in my head, and an entire year of happiness lost. All for what?

* * *

Nothing. Holding a grudge is a "powerless" activity. And for every minute you're holding one power is oozing from your pores.

Reclaim your power...*Forgive.*

Introspection

Are you holding any grudges? With whom? How often is that person occupying your mind; creating negative energy in your body? What ways are you benefiting from the grudge?

Loving Yourself with Self-Love
By Makeeta House

When you get to a point in your life where you understand the power of LOVE, then you have joined many individuals who choose to be happy! Not only do we want love, but we also take detours to love ourselves, also tending to wait for a while to acknowledge when something is wrong in our lives and our relationships. I have learned that the sooner we get into agreement with the problem, the sooner you will move past life's challenges. Who likes a challenge? Unless it's a benefit "drinking water challenge" or "prayer challenge" you plan with your girlfriends, most want nothing to do with the valleys of life. But today, I advocate a challenge that will push you past your comfort zone but will guarantee to bring the best out of you. Are you ready to love yourself more than you ever have before? Get by yourself and take steps to re-build a love for the areas you have let go

● ● ●

or now needing to create! Never allow yourself to be intimidated by years of neglect due to how your journey has been in your life. You may not even feel you have a lifestyle at all; this is your time to work towards building the personal love into your life to build with the others on many levels you have put aside to keep your life together.

Are you ready to dream while you are wide awake? Visualize yourself living a life that honors "YOU" in a healthy and mindful way. We often honor others instead of ourselves. To set boundaries, you will need first to say unapologetically you are going to honor yourself with a new beginning of loving yourself. Can you close your eyes and see the person that you are capable of becoming? Now, are you ready to acknowledge that you have not loved yourself, mindfully? If you're ready to move forward now, say out loud a few times… "I want to love myself completely; I am ready to make changes now." How does working towards stabilizing your lifestyle with self-love feel? With a simple but powerful statement, you have just moved one step closer to the women who now work towards not letting their emotions interfere with their enlargement to greatness.

Guilt. If most of us follow the "self-neglect" thread back to the beginning, we will likely find guilt is the culprit.

Even when we may not be at fault, many women often feel so guilty for wrongdoings, and we become the sacrificial lamb who takes all the blame when things don't work out or don't go the way we planned. For example, in the case of a divorce, most women walk away thinking it's completely their fault, even when it's not. And as they take all the blame on themselves and too many times, they are unable to forgive themselves. Guilt is just one of the many emotions that lack of self-love is what often leads to the feelings of hopelessness. Here it is important to understand that if you don't love yourself and learn to forgive yourself even when you are partially at fault, you won't be able to live a happy and content life. You'll always find yourself unhappy, restless, hopeless, and depressed.

Self-love, hope, and respect are extremely important to move on with life even when bad things happen. Let's take a deeper dive to understand the importance of self-love and hope; and how exactly are these two factors linked to better love yourself.

You see, self-love like the word itself suggests is the act of valuing your happiness and personal well-being. It can be best described as the acceptance of one's self by providing unconditional support and care with compassion. The act of self-love enables you to view yourself as worthy, valuable, and a person who deserves happiness. However, when we find ourselves in the wrong act, especially when it happened unintentionally, we often fail to forgive ourselves. As we are unable to forgive ourselves, we find it extremely hard to love ourselves. And this is exactly why we at times:

√ Beat own self up with harsh self-talk and cruel words;

√ Set own self for failure by keeping unrealistic expectations;

√ Deprive us of things that we truly deserve with a self-sabotaging behavior; and

√ Abuse our own body by making bad choices or neglecting our needs.

All these kinds of behaviors can wreak havoc on our physical and mental health, career, and relationship. To avoid this and to live a happy life, it is important to self-love. Remember if you don't love yourself and don't respect yourself; nobody else will. Many people think that self-love is a natural thing, but as I have noticed, it is not easy to self-love as we think it is. Taking care of yourself can start great while you are young. However, it begins to fade away as you grow older, especially when you faced with betrayal or another kind of life challenges. You may find yourself asking questions like:

√ How did I get to this place of comfort and lose my ability to self-care?

√ When did life dwindle and become dull?

Sometimes we start off as leaders, but over time, we lose ourselves in the journey. But if we hold on to the promises of God, God will always work to get you out of an area that deems to be hopeless.

Hope is the opposite of hopelessness. Noticing a person or yourself as hopeless is one of the most meaningful targets to get an individual healthy in a propelling way. If you don't have any hope what will happen is that negative thoughts will consume you. You will need more attention to the matter than a bad day so always allow yourself to do a self-check and love yourself first. We hear it often, but its best practiced in scripture 37, Jesus declared, "Love the Lord your God with all your heart and with all your soul and with all your mind."

Loving yourself assists you with how you love others. Second-guessing how to love the next person you meet to knowing you have more than enough love for yourself and others if supplied by God above and given out properly. Mistreatment of love can happen but allowing your thoughts to know it's a gift to love, a scripture to reference is 1 Cor 13:13 "And now these three remain: faith, hope, and love. But the greatest of them is love."

You have to trust God in loving yourself and others. He has a place for you. It shows His unconditional love in our everyday walk of life. I personally have had to get into the word and study how did Jesus love and still need the grace to love as He does.

Gratitude is another area of self-love. Staying hopeful and thankful to how you know He is with you. He still has goals for you after the forgiveness has taken place. He also knows you are going to need to work on your behavioral habits to have wholeness.

√ How do you react after an incident occurs that you do not care for?

√ Do you hold on to it, or do you forgive to have hope for the situation to turn around?

√ Do you wait for more others to respond first, or are you first to respond?

√ How can next time be better in forgiving quickly?

Now allow me to share with you some more amazing steps to practicing self-love.

To begin with, I suggest you practice self-care. Self-care is a great way to get started when it comes to loving yourself. You can do this by doing small yet meaningful things like:

✓ Getting enough sleep which is great for your body as it helps the body feel revitalize and energized;

✓ Doing yoga as it helps provide peace of mind;

✓ Drinking water;

✓ Hanging out with friends and family for a relaxing and joyful time.

If you have noticed, all of the activities that I have mentioned above are related to yourself. And needless to say, are focused towards your personal well-being. Often at times we get so busy and acquired in our daily and hectic routine, and in others that we forget to give time to and pay attention to ourselves.

At times being too self-critical, we end up sabotaging our happiness and putting ourselves down even when it is not that big of an issue in the first place. If this negativity for ourselves is not controlled; it can damage us badly. All this can lower our self-esteem, confidence, and often when negative emotions become so extreme that it can even lead to suicidal thoughts. Start early with self-love, begin not to delay any time to believe it cannot happen to you. As you maintain a happy mindset, you can prevent how you want the outcome of your mental health can be stronger than. I enjoy speaking accomplishments to myself, we all have heard to celebrate, but how about not feeling guilty on how you really went for a goal conquered it, and you want to remember the accomplishment more than worry.

Women can casually worry on every level of life but forget to remain focus on how great they are becoming. When you decide, I am not just a woman with a purpose but actually, a woman that sets goals to get to the purpose, you then begin to love yourself effortlessly. It's ok, to not overthink and love what you have done when you're in a place you don't like what's around you. So how do you do that?

By acknowledging a few helpful tips! Grab on to when you were at the highest points in your life and do not be afraid of doing it! Yes, we know the scenario where we see an athlete replay where the championship was one, but how about you acknowledge your accomplishments on the scale that you were created to become the women you are today.

Another tip finds out why you choose to neglect loving yourself by yourself. If you tend to be around friends and want to start a conversation with your worries instead of the last week or month you managed every area right, then you are choosing to low ball your greatness. We all use terms to get back in the game to bounce back, but the next level is to acknowledge yourself at whatever age you are to be as great as you were affirmed from someone that comes into your life such as the spouse you are waiting on or the parent to tell you to go for it.

An individual usually gets there by others acknowledging their goals, but I want to break the standard and began to let you know you can be happy in the beginning, middle, and after your goals are met. We work hard to show our best dress, but we also want to get to the best place of happiness in working towards how we desire to love ourselves in the middle of relocating, finding a mate, or wanting more funds in the bank. Now how do you work on your place of happiness? You have to define happiness for yourself!

Your intentions to be happy may need to be re-evaluated with loving sisters who can support you on the journey. Love how you are working on yourself and not how you failed. The word failure is a memorable one that hits the heart of a person, but as long as you have breath, you can re-write your story to a balance that can bring love into your life.

One place of loving yourself is breathing in beautiful affirming words to yourself as you choose to look at yourself differently. Enjoy saying how you want to see yourself daily. Add reminders if you are a person who may forget this new way of thinking or if you have never committed to writing out a plan of action. This is very important for many women, the technique is becoming aware of who you are, now acknowledging that somewhere in the middle you have had goals or desires to get back to you, want to begin an area you never did start and now you are constantly repeating it in your mind with no thought of wanting to give in to the fact nothing has taken place. If that's you, start again!

Chose to now allow yourself the freedom in self-love to find out the right wellness pattern to start, where you want to begin is important. Then write out a timeline and a plan to discover how you can add in goals to lead your behavior positively. Be aware you will get interruptions but still staying confident is so much easier than dreading till the next lifecycle of choices become available and aware to you. To nurture self-love, you need to spend quality time with yourself. Some activities set time aside for daily mindfulness practices like deep breathing, progressive muscle relaxation techniques, and meditation. Even if you take 15 to 30 minutes for these activities, you'll feel a world of a difference. Stay strong and want more in life. Figure out where you may not have been taught properly to be your best version. Remain teachable and understand needing help is a great step to start to work on your self-love. Of course, 20 years ago, the term self-love was not used as much; however, it is our responsibility to take care of ourselves and love ourselves regardless of what's happening in our lives. This truth hurts because of the lack of the village we so need more in our cities to help those who do have bad health reports or new babies to raise and still be at their best health. However, with each individual deciding to desire to love themselves, we can now reach more women, not in a helpless way but a true motivated foundation for a better life. Thrive more by loving you; you will see a new part of you awaken. I can assure you that happiness and mental peace you can't put a price tag on these factors and are not easy to find and can't be bought—they are priceless. Therefore, to find inner peace and happiness, you need to understand yourself more by connecting with yourself.

About the Author

Makeeta House is known as "The coach's coach" because she goes beyond just coaching others. She brings 20 years of career experience in workforce training and management. Makeeta House earned her BA in Human Relations and Management from Mid-America Nazarene University. She is a certified Master Life Coach, a Christian Coach, and

Health and Wellness Coach. Makeeta is the host of "Stepping into Wholeness" on 95.3 FM radio. She is the operating owner of Abilities Influence Measure Coaching and the Non-Profit Wishful Wellness Network.

To learn more about Makeeta visit
www.wishfulwellness.com
For inquiries email lifecoachinfluencer@gmail.com or call 816-585-9526
Connect with Makeeta (FaceBook) @WishfulWellness and on Instagram @MakeetaHouse

Power Booster #6
By Cathy Upshire

*"If someone has a negative opinion of you, it's okay.
People have a right to their own opinion, and you have a
right to disagree. Question is...do you?"*

- Cathy Upshire, *"Woman Find Thyself"*

When someone has a negative opinion of us, it is nearly impossible to change their view. So, don't. We must allow people to feel however they want and not take that on as our problem or issue. It's only a problem if we agree with their assessment.

I was talking to a group of women at a transitional housing facility for women coming out of prison when one of the ladies raised her hand and said one of the ladies there called her fat. She went on to say, "That thing really hurt me. I mean...I didn't sleep for three days!" So, I said, "What does her calling you fat have to do with you?" She looked puzzled. Then I said, "Will all the fat people in this room, please stand up." Eighty percent of us stood. "Look at all these fat people." I blurted at the women who stood. "Did I hurt your feelings by calling you all fat?" "No!" They bellowed.

"It wasn't the fact that this woman called you fat that had you losing sleep," I continued, "because she was telling the truth. You are fat. It was the way she said it. She said it in a way as to imply you were *disgusting* because you were fat. And the reason it hurt was that somewhere deep down inside, you agree." I could tell she was having an "Ah-Ha!" moment. "You can call me fat all day long," I went on, "and you know what I'd say, *"Well—I know that!" And your point is? LOL,* I don't see my weight as being disgusting, and you can't insult me by implying it is. It's only a problem if I agree. And I don't. I am beautiful; all 178 pounds of me.

<u>Introspection</u>

Are there people in your life who have negative opinions of you? What opinions do they have? Do you agree with their assessment? If you do, you have work to do.

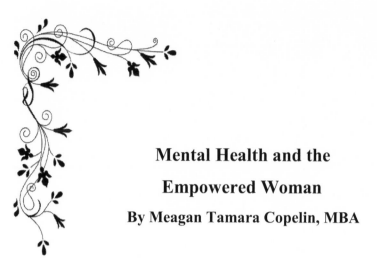

Mental Health and the
Empowered Woman
By Meagan Tamara Copelin, MBA

"All women are powerful, we are powerful at birth, but sometimes our life experiences have a way of making us relinquish our power."

As a young girl growing up in the city of New Orleans, I was always determined to be the very best and to never give up despite my obstacles. In fact, my aunts and uncles nicknamed me "Maybe Tomorrow" instead of my given name, Meagan Tamara! My great-grandmother Anna Copelin, who passed away when I was three years of age, nursed me back to health with her tender love and care, called me Mee-Mee. I don't remember my great-grandmother much, who most called Mother Anna, but I do know that she cared for me when my young parents could not. My mom gave birth to me as a young teenager, and my dad just twenty years old. I was raised by my great-grandmother for the first three years of my life, not because she wanted to but because she needed to. Even as a premature baby, I had so much fight in me. My great-grandmother Anna, and my great-grandfather Daniel Copelin, who we called Granddaddy Copelin were full of love. The greatest memories I shared with my granddaddy were us sitting at the kitchen table eating ginger snaps, but he ate his ginger snaps with hot dog links. I still smile, thinking about how my granddaddy enjoyed a snack that I found unpleasant.

I loved spending time with my granddaddy. He was extremely funny, and I miss him and Mother Anna dearly. As for my birth mother, she was in and out of my life until the age of eight, but she was never physically and emotionally there. At the age of eight, my mother walked away from her responsibilities, and I didn't see her until again. I was 21 years of age. It was clear that her priorities were being in the streets versus being a mother to me. Not only were my birth mother young and immature, but she was also addicted to drugs. Needless to say, growing up with a mother like this was rough. My father left my life when I was around seven years old or so, and as a child, I didn't understand why.

After Mother Anna passed away, I didn't have my caretaker. I didn't realize I would soon face hell.

As a child, school was always an important part of my life. As a matter of fact, I can still remember the school song from George Washington Elementary School, 20 years later. Don't laugh (lol). I take great pride in remembering that song! I loved to learn, but school wasn't always a fun place to be. I was bullied a lot in elementary school because of the way I appeared to other kids. I didn't have the best of clothes and at times would attend school with the same clothes from the previous day or wear the same outfit for the entire week. Despite these unpleasant realities, I wanted to be at school as much as possible as my home life was no walk in the park. School was a place I was guaranteed two meals per day during the week. School was a place I could wash my face, body, and hands. School was my safe haven. George Washington Elementary School played a major role in who I am today.

No matter how much I was bullied, I still went to school Monday to Friday. I was at peace in school because I was able to escape the torment of being sexually abused by my mom's boyfriend. After school, I would go home and crawl under the house to complete my homework because that was the only way I could escape my problems for a few more hours before dark arrived. At the age of 8 years, I was dealing with issues that no child should ever have to face. I should have been playing with barbie dolls and eating dinner at the table with my family, but I was dealing with grown people issues. Despite or maybe because of these unspeakable challenges in my young life, I made a promise to myself at the age of 10 years old that I would achieve the highest degree attainable, no matter where I was in life. I was determined to overcome those obstacles I was facing at that time in my life. Understandably so, during this time, I started to become depressed. Of course, at this age, I didn't know or understand what the word depressed even meant. I just knew I was facing issues that were not normal for a child. I kept pushing forward because I had goals to accomplish, and I wanted to make sure they were achieved. I could not give up on myself even when others had given up on me. I knew the person I would talk to while I was under the house was protecting me. I had angels all around me, and God was positioning me to become a strong woman for the future.

During my childhood, I lived with several relatives, and during this time, I still felt unwanted and rejected by many. I suffered from various mental health disorders, such as anxiety, OCD, PTSD, and bipolar disorder. I once became so depressed that I scratched my face until the skin started to peel off. My Aunt decided it was time for me to seek professional help to deal with the trauma I was facing. Here I was in high school, still wetting the bed. That's not normal is what I was told. People will think I am crazy, is what I commented to my Aunt after my first visit to the psychiatrist. I can't possibly be crazy if I seek professional help, right?

After feeling hopeless and worthless for many years, I attempted suicide a few years ago. I was in a state of depression and suffering from a personality disorder. I was angry at myself, and the world for being birth to parents who I felt didn't give a F*** about me. I was MAD! I was frustrated, and I didn't want to live in this world anymore. I felt hopeless. The night I decided to end my life by taking 70 pills was the night that changed my life. It was dark, gloomy, and rainy outside. I was alone in the apartment I shared with my roommate. My friend decided that she wanted to visit, so I left the door unlocked for her. The feeling of helplessness overcame me, and I completely forgot she was coming. She found me and immediately called for help, and I was transported to the hospital. GOD was protecting me. Mother Anna and Granddaddy Copelin were watching over me. Once at the hospital, the nursing staff attempted to pump my stomach, but I fought them and told them to let me die. They refused. At some point, I punched a nurse in the face and kicked a security guard in the stomach for attempting to save my life. The hospital staff had to handcuff my arms and legs to the bed so that they could continue to save my life. All I could hear was Mother Anna saying, "Girl, if you don't keep still and let these people save you, we are going to have a problem." My angel was still protecting me. She was the same woman who nursed me back to health as a premature baby, so of course, she wanted to continue to nurture me and love me. I was grateful for her presence and knew I could not give up.

After finally stabilizing me, I was informed by the nursing staff that I was being transported to another area in the hospital for further monitoring. After about an hour of being in the emergency room, I was approached by two individuals in green uniforms. They informed me they were there to transport me to another facility. I was confused. I was previously told that I would be transported to another section of the hospital. All I knew was that the situation appeared strange, and I was being transported in a bed that didn't appear normal in an ambulance that looked quite different than the usual. They were there to transport me to an inpatient mental health facility. Dang, here I felt like I had major issues yet again. There was no way I was going to stay in a place confined to a room 20 hours a day, wearing a straitjacket. Yes, I wore a straitjacket while housed in a mental health facility. Ummmm, I don't think so. All I could ask myself was, "Is this is a dream?" I had to quickly talk to God and ask Him to get me out of this situation. I promise I will never attempt suicide again. Well, GOD had other plans. I was a patient at the facility for 6 days. Those 6 days felt like 60 days. I didn't want to be there, but I needed to be there at that moment in my life. I was determined to change my life and way of thinking, no matter what. God had always been by my side, and I didn't want to fail him. I wanted Anna and Daniel Copelin to be proud of me.

Here I was on my way to becoming a successful career woman, but deep inside, I was angry. I didn't love myself. I looked at myself daily in the mirror and tore myself apart. I didn't like me. I had major issues.

Mental illness is REAL. The key is to get treatment as soon as you recognize what your problems are. The stigma surrounding mental illness is prevalent, and people are hesitant to call diagnoses illnesses because they don't want to admit that it's an ailment.

If it had not been for the opportunity to dream, I would not be sharing my story coming from where I came from. I didn't have the correct support system, and many people laughed at me due to my illness, especially family members. Many doubted me and told me I would be just like my mom, a drug-addicted teen mom with no education and a laundry list of a criminal record. I am proud to say I am neither the list of things people said I would be.

Because of the way I looked to others, there was no way I was dealing with mental health disorders, as one of my cousins stated. I was told, I am strong. You are just hurt and dealing with pain, they would say. African Americans don't typically deal with mental health disorders, right? WRONG.

According to the US HHS Office of Minority Health, adult African Americans are more likely to have feelings of sadness, hopelessness, and worthlessness than are adult whites. African Americans of all ages are more likely to be victims of serious violent crime than are non-Hispanic whites, making them more likely to meet the diagnostic criteria for post-traumatic stress disorder (PTSD). Let's not concern ourselves with stigma and understand when it is time to seek and ask for help.

I am, however, grateful for my past because my past has made me a stronger woman, an EMPOWERED woman.

I make no excuses. I can stand strong when I face adversity. I realized that I was not how others saw me. I wanted to change my life and be the girl who decided to go for it. It makes no sense to dream if you are going to dream small. My dreams have always been bright and full of color.

Let's face it; I was dealing with several mental issues and had no clue how to cope until I implemented the strategies listed below.

I am presenting myself to you as a product of a drug-addicted mother and an absent father. I was able to manage many of the mental health disorders I once faced because I never gave up on myself. I still struggle with mental health but with patient and love for myself, the days have gotten a whole lot better. As of today, I am currently pursuing the dream I set for myself at the age of 10 years old and will be graduating with my doctorate in May 2020. Dr. Meagan Tamara Copelin has goals to accomplish and lives to change. I can't stop now.

Here are a few ways I was able to cope with and manage my clinical depression over the years:

1. I had to learn to **FORGIVE** myself and others. Through forgiveness, the miracle of transformation happened within me. The magic of forgiveness is a big part of what

fuels my passion for my work with **"The Forgiveness Brand."** Once I was able to experience the magic of forgiveness, everything got easier for me: life, letting go, acceptance, forgiveness, and loving myself.

2. I started to journal and read my BIBLE. I started to spend more time with GOD and eventually was able to accept myself as I was and who GOD saw me for. I was able to trust the process and understand my purpose in life. I started to feel refreshed and empowered. Here I was with a new opportunity to live my life at the fullest. **I was at PEACE. I am at PEACE.**

3. I had to begin to understand the power to enact real change in the way I was thinking, behaving, and coping daily. I had to put in the work **EVERYDAY.**

4. I made a list of "my people." I consider myself an introvert at times, so I had to build a detailed list of people who I could trust, and I knew who would not judge me. **SURROUND YOURSELF WITH SUPPORTIVE PEOPLE AND LET GO OF NEGATIVE PEOPLE, family included.**

5. I started to follow a strict schedule. I started to take control of my life and didn't allow unnecessary interferences to get in the way. I felt good saying, "NO."

6. I started to practice **SELF CARE**. I had to get my mind, body, soul, and inner peace right. I basically had to check myself and tell myself, get it all the way together.

7. I sought **COUNSELING**. You are not crazy because you are asking for help. A counselor is there to assist and not judge. A counselor is at times easiest to speak with than people who are closest to you.

I am happy being the best version of myself. That little girl who hid under the house had big dreams, and now I have become a woman with great vision.

REMEMBER: A woman who has everything has nothing, YET a woman who believes in herself has everything.

For additional help and support with your concerns, please speak with a licensed counselor or therapist TODAY.

About the Author

Meagan is an international speaker, author, success coach, mentor, and podcaster. Meagan's passion is to become a trailblazing voice for young girls and women worldwide.

Drawing on her own experiences of abuse, rejection, and abandonment, Meagan uses her words to encourage others to build a home within themselves; to love, live, and create fearlessly. Her tremendous projects and efforts have helped her to be featured on several platforms for the purpose of empowering women to tell their story from struggle to success and live up to their full potential.

Meagan Copelin Global www.MeaganCopelin.com
For inquiries email: sheinspires@meagancopelin.com
Connect with Meagan (Facebook, Instagram, Twitter) @MeaganCopelinGlobal

Power Booster #7
By Cathy Upshire

"I want people to love me for who I am."
Well, who are you? If you're not being who you really are,
we can't love you for WHO you are. So, will the real
you please stand up so we can love her.

- Cathy Upshire, *"Woman Find Thyself"*

So, I finally got the courage to do the unthinkable after not being able to for decades. STAND. Not just stand, but in my own skin. The skin some weren't going embrace or approve of or even like for that matter. The skin that was ready to take its place in *front* of the curtain, because it wasn't born to be in the shadow's backstage. The skin I'd decided I wasn't going to dumb down or quiet anymore. Yes—I STOOD; hands shaking; knees knocking; heart racing. I STOOD. I stood to attract those who'd loved me for who I was because I was so tired of being an inferior version of myself.

I STOOD, and I waited. And I was okay waiting because for the first time in a long time I took the lead in my *own* life; deciding who I wanted in *my* life and not waiting for someone else to decide if they wanted me in theirs. I STOOD as a declaration to the world that I am *enough* and that there are those who will be drawn to my light like a moth in the night.

I STOOD for those who didn't *care* I thought I was cute (hadn't really thought about it), but what was I *supposed* to think. I stood for those who didn't *care* I was smart because they found my conversations thought provoking and intellectually stimulating. I STOOD for those who didn't *care,* I knew what I knew, and as *much* as I knew because they received inspiration from the fruit of my lips.

So yes—I STOOD, I waited, they came—not those who wanted me to slouch my shoulders or dim my light because they felt overshadowed by my radiant glow—No, just those who *wanted* to be in my life—because they were attracted to *my* light in all of its glory. And now I'm free because the woman inside of me—held captive to the skin of an imposter—found the courage to STAND; not just stand, but in her *own* skin.

Introspection

In what ways are you showing up in the world? Is it the *real* you? Do you even know who the *real* you are? Who is she? Are you talkative or quiet; are you "bossy" or deferential? Do you prefer to be in front of the curtain or backstage?

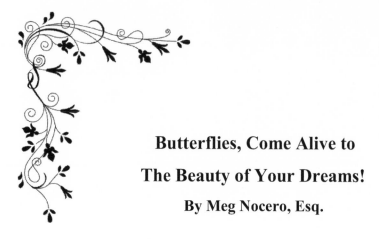

Butterflies, Come Alive to
The Beauty of Your Dreams!
By Meg Nocero, Esq.

"You were born with wings.
Why prefer to crawl through life?"
-Rumi

Are you ready to embark on an unforgettable adventure of wonder discovering the keys that will lead you to experience more bliss in your life? I am here to challenge the notion that you are stuck in a life that falls far short of where you want to be. Here and now, as you read this chapter, I invite you to begin a life-changing journey of self-discovery to recover a sense of meaning and fully realize your personal passions coming alive to the beauty of your dreams. It is time to say YES! to the journey towards bliss by starting to pay attention to your inner voice guided by these simple instructions set out by the late poet Mary Oliver

• • •

on how to live a conscious life: *pay attention, be astonished, and tell about it.*

Are you ready?

First, align with the present moment by de-cluttering your mind of those things that no longer serve you and pay attention to ideas born in your childlike imagination. Next, get astonished by the opportunity to embrace the amazing unknown by getting in touch with your dreams so that you can visualize all that is possible for your life. There, start anew to live from a place of consciousness where magic and miracles reside. Breathe deeply again and slow down the pace a little bit. Pause with intention, taking in all that life has to offer one day at a time. Lastly, tell a new story as you wake up and begin to rejoice in the something wonderful that is always about to happen. By introducing these instructions, you will be empowered by your dreams and come alive to choices so that you can make a positive difference in your small corner of this world and have a ripple effect on others, one person at a time.

Revisit that Child at Play and Find Your Purpose...

As a child, do you remember playing and connecting with others on a very basic level, conscious of what brought you great joy, staying present in the moment discovering what it had to offer? Ask yourself, what did you naturally love to do. I loved to draw, dance, sing, and play with my sisters and friends as much as I could all day long. As a very creative little girl with dramatic flair, I set out confidently embracing life. Somehow, I knew in my heart that I could do anything that I put my mind to. I believed and dwelt in possibility. Engaging my imagination, I used to sit for hours writing fantastic stories. There, I could create different and wonderful characters who existed in magical places and faraway lands, ready to be explored. Fascinated by color, I would draw and paint bright and happy images bringing vibrancy to my world. I loved to design beautiful, elegant gowns that I imagined I would someday wear to galas that took place in gloriously decorated ballrooms. And, my family, the audience I shared my work with, delighted in it and returned positive feedback, proudly acknowledging my creativity.

Yet, things did change as I grew into an awkward adolescent and young adult. I had a mouth full of metal and wore thick glasses matched only by a nerdy haircut and extra girth around the middle. Each day in middle school was a challenge where I dealt with bullies whose incessant teasing highlighted my flaws and less than attractive appearance. I quickly lost interest in school, and my grades suffered. I ended up retreating into my own little world resorting to food to numb myself out for not fitting in and feeling like an overall failure. There, my life as a happy go lucky, creative child began to disappear before my eyes. It was replaced by the belief that I needed approval from others to feel worthy.

That destructive belief remained with me throughout the rest of my formative years up until adulthood when I grew tired of never meeting up to impossible standards. It was no longer satisfying for me to continue going through the motions of a legal career surrounded by a chain of command that did not align with my soul. I could no longer maintain appearances of keeping up with a full-time job while not spending enough time with my children. I was just surviving, when I knew all I wanted to do was thrive. And, I wasted a lot of time and many years trying to get recognition and prove myself worthy by doing things that brought me joy but were not valued by others.

Once I declared to the Divine that I was ready to change my beliefs, only then could my life start to change. Gradually, I decided I had enough of judgment and criticism and woke up to my own beauty within. I finally dared to take care of myself by placing my dreams first. It was time to stop being a victim to any overarching paradigm of world beliefs that replaced my own desires with what I believed were the expectations of others. It was time to get silent and turn off the external chatter of the world so that I could reconnect to that inner child and get intentional. That is when I started to clarify the yearnings of my soul. And with awareness and reflection, I returned to a conscious state revisiting that child at play, so that frustrations could fall away and a sense of purpose returned.

Pay Attention! All the World's a Stage for Your Dreams to Unfold

Today is the day for you to unveil that magical dream of yours. And to match the grandness of your dreams, you must make its debut sparkle and shine! Dressed in the most exquisite of gowns, you place that beautiful crown upon your head and walk confidently out from stage left to where it all unfolds. Unapologetically choosing a path that is most aligned with your authentic self, you take center stage waiting for the curtain to rise so that a new exciting chapter of your life can begin. How did you get here? You got intentional. Set out your vision. You believed in the possible. And, most importantly, you changed the way you see the world, and the world you saw started to change. You paid attention and said yes to the opportunities that prepared you well for this moment in time. Now that you're here, you boldly place your hands on both sides of your hips empowering yourself in what speaker, Amy Cuddy coined the "superwoman pose" and repeat over and over again those "I AM" affirmations that have taken you so far. When the house lights go down, the room falls silent, and you wait for the orchestra to start playing the musical soundtrack that is tailor-made just for you. As if on cue, when you take a deep breath, the curtain slowly goes up, and the bright white spotlight shines down onto where you stand. The audience waits with bated breath as if this is the moment that they've all been waiting for. A drumroll ensues…a voice from above announces over the loudspeaker, "Introducing (insert your name)." Bubbling over with excitement, you step into your calling and take your place in this world and announce why you are here!

Empowered and ready to start your own show, you may ask, how do I get to that place on that stage? The answer is simple: *you are already there*! You were born with a purpose, a calling, and big dreams. It is entirely up to you to wake up, get curious, pay attention, and seek out the opportunities to create the life you want. I am here to tell you that you've had the power all along; everything that has happened until this point is synchronistic and serves a greater purpose. There are no mistakes in life; your show must go on.

Reflecting on my own journey, my educational opportunities continue to open many doors. From learning to speak four languages to earning a master's degree in International Studies, I traveled the world and moved around the country, connecting with many people along the way. As a federal immigration prosecutor for over 19 years, I fine-tuned my listening skills, learned to articulate myself in any setting clearly, and enhanced my writing skills. By spear-heading my office's legal intern program, I formally coached and mentored over 300 law students over the years, both professionally and personally. And, I was trained well, earning certifications as an instructor with the agency's mentoring program as well as with the Federal Law Enforcement Training Center in Glenco, Georgia. When the time came to take my life journey in a new direction, I was better able to catapult bigger dreams because of the solid foundation that I built.

While there was a point in time when I believed that I was stuck and would never have any opportunities to reach my full potential, I felt powerless. Fear of the unknown kept me in a job that provided a good living but no longer aligned with my passion. It felt like I traded in my golden "tiara" for golden "handcuffs." While I resigned myself to suck it up, my life was speaking in whispers that were only getting louder, and my soul beckoned to find a way to be free. Not able to think outside of the well-crafted box, I grew internally impatient with my circumstances, angrier and unsettled. Yet, externally, I smiled never showing any signs of falling apart.

When my mother passed away in 2011 as a result of her battle with breast cancer, the whispers turned into a ringing, *tinnitus*, that forced me to wake up and face life. Before she died, she shared two bits of wisdom: stress will kill you and have no regrets at the end of your days. On the verge of a nervous breakdown, I heeded her final words. I chose to figure out ways to limit the impact of stress with the best healing tools for me to navigate the grieving process; then, I decided to take a leap of faith exploring a new career path as an educator, writer, speaker and coach so I would have no regrets too. That is when I decided it was time to take my own center stage and announce to the world my magical dream. I was ready to inspire others and empower generations to come alive to the beauty of their dreams by realizing my own. What happened next was amazing!

Thrive Girl, Thrive!

Be astonished and then tell all about it! Therein lies the magic for dreams to come alive...

On October 25, 2014, one of my biggest dreams came true. It was the second day of Oprah's *Live the Life You Want* conference at the American Airlines Arena in Miami, Florida and I had tickets to go. My energy was high, and after seeing Oprah on stage the night before, I was looking forward to seeing her again with the rest of the speakers. As we found our seats on the arena floor again, many were dancing to the DJ's high energy music and buzzing around with enthusiasm.

Two days before the Miami event, I had a dream. In it, I was sitting in the audience at the Oscars chatting with Steven Spielberg and his wife, Kate Capshaw. After a short time, I looked up and saw Oprah in the crowd coming my way. When she was about two feet away, she stopped, looked at me, then turned and walked off. I remembered wanting to scream, "Come Back! Why are you walking away?" I woke up in a panic, having to convince myself that it was not a premonition but only a dream. So, without ruminating further, I let it go. Besides, for the entire month before, I had been visualizing that I would actually meet Oprah on stage in front of the entire crowd. Just like when I met Bob Barker in 1991 on the *Price is Right,* in my visual

Oprah would call to me and invite me to join her by saying, "Come on Down!" Without hesitation, I would obediently climb up on stage next to her. As a student of the *law of attraction*, I focused and got excited about this unfolding as I knew the importance that emotions have on manifesting dreams. Believing that harnessing the power of my emotions would provide the momentum to create a reality I wanted, I fixated only on the possibility of my visualization coming to light.

At the Miami event, sitting next to my good friend Karyn, dressed in a "not to be missed" canary yellow jacket, wearing a tiara, I was spotted by my friend Mari who somehow made her way down to the floor from the nosebleed section to find me. And, serendipitously there was an open seat right next to me. Surrounded by my friends and with the high energy in the room, I was ready for something magical to happen. Suddenly the high energy music stopped, and Deepak Chopra took center stage with Oprah, encouraging all of us to join in the meditation. At the end of the meditation, as calm music continued to play, Oprah asked all of us to journal on what we wished for our loved ones. Then "O" descended on the audience to pick people to share their answers on stage. Because I was sitting right in front of her path, Oprah was heading for me. She stood right in front of me, looked me in the eye, and smiled; I was bursting with excitement. Then, she glanced at Mari sitting to my right, read her journal entry, smiled, said, "I like you," grabbed Mari's hand, and walked away.

My stomach immediately dropped! What just happened? Then, I suddenly remembered my previous dream with Steven Spielberg and coupled that with the message Oprah shared the night before about how she got her part in the movie *The Color Purple*. Oprah said she desperately wanted to play the character Sofia and worried that her "dream role" was slipping away. That was until her life whispered for her to trust and let it go. When she did, Spielberg called her that same evening, and she got the role. That was it. The secret to abundance is not having a mindset of scarcity. Ask, believe, and trust the process to receive. There are no mistakes in life. As soon as I let go of my fear of not meeting her, I, too, turned to the possibility again. Not even minutes after I did, I heard Mari on stage say my name followed by Oprah asking, "Where's Meg?" Then, like Bob Barker, she invited me to come on down. As my visualization unfolded in real-time, I climbed up the stairs from the left, hugged Mari, and took my place center stage waving to the audience alongside Oprah, telling her how much I loved her, even going into an "ugly cry." Oprah smiled and told me not to cry, or it would ruin the photos. I had so much fun up there with her!

Astonished and thankful, my "impossible dream" came true in an amazing way! That was the first real glimpse into the life I wanted, and I have not looked back since. Today, I am on a new life and career path, embracing the uncertainty rather than running from it. And, perhaps for you, these keys are exactly what you need to hear to live a more blissful life, there are no coincidences that you are reading this now.

- Pay attention
- Be astonished
- Tell all about it!

It is time for you to reconnect to your inner child, take your rightful place at center stage in this world, and get excited! For sure, the Divine will keep sending you positive signs when you do. Your audience is waiting for you to unveil your magical dream and show up as authentically as you can in line with its beauty. Take a bow and come alive. Then, accept the thunderous applause acknowledging the beginnings of a great transformation as you start to fly, becoming the most amazing butterfly too!

About the Author

Meg Nocero, Esq. is an attorney (former federal prosecutor) inspirational speaker, certified empowerment coach, educator, and award-winning author. She holds a BA in Spanish, with a concentration in Italian from Boston College; an MA in International Affairs from the University of Miami; and a JD from St. Thomas University School of Law. She holds certifications with the Department of Homeland Security Mentoring Program, as a Federal Law Enforcement Training Center instructor, as a Professional Coach with the Institute for Professional Excellence in Coaching and is an accredited ACC through the International Coaching Federation. She is currently pursuing a Certificate in Happiness Studies led by Harvard Professor Dr. Tal Ben-Shahar.

As a part of The Meg Nocero Network, Meg runs Butterflies & Bliss, LLC, founded a non-profit called S.H.I.N.E. Networking Inc. that provides educational scholarships to young innovative leaders, is a Love Button Global Movement Ambassador, and a contributing author for Amy Butler's on-line magazine publication called <u>Blossom</u>. She has been published on various media sites including

MSNBC, The Boston Herald, CBS, AJC, ABC News, and many more.

She is an award-winning author of *The Magical Guide to Bliss, Daily Keys to Unlock Your Dreams, Spirit & Inner Bliss,* of her memoir of transformation, *"Beautiful Butterfly, How Grief Enveloped Me, Transformed Me, and Freed Me to Live the Life I Want!"* and a how-to on starting an affirmation practice called *"Sparkle & Shine, 108 M.A.N.T.R.A.s to Brighten Your Day and Lighten Your Way".*

Butterflies & Bliss, LLC www.MegNocero.com
For inquiries email megnocero@me.com
Connect with Meg (FaceBook, Instagram, Twitter, LinkedIn)
@MegNocero

Power Booster #8
By Cathy Upshire

"There's always someone to blame for the messes in our life. If we are to reclaim our power, our hunger to do so must outweigh whose fault it was, who started it or who should pay; we must be willing to accept the role we played in the mess."

- Cathy Upshire, *"Woman Find Thyself"*

If we can learn to accept our role in some of the situations, we find ourselves in; even some of the more painful ones, we're less likely to find ourselves in those situations again. And there's almost always someone else to blame, "She did this...and he did that"; the vocabulary of a victim--he, she, they and them. But if someone else was responsible for 95% of the mess, be accountable for your five.

Being accountable for the role we played in the messes in our lives doesn't mean we're blaming ourselves for them, it only means we're taking inventory of the situation, determining what we could've done differently, accepting responsibility for not doing what we should've done in the first place and vowing to do better the next time the situation arises.

I've never felt more powerful than when I took responsibility for my own life and its outcomes. As long as we assume the posture of "the victim" or "the wounded one," I was left with the open wounded to show for it. I'm more than happy to take responsibility for the role I played because when I do my power and sense of well-being remains in tack.

* * *

Introspection

Think of a situation you were in that resulted in a big mess; one you may have even gotten hurt in. Did you accept responsibility for the role you played in the mess, or did you assume the role of "the wounded one?"

More Than a Womb

By Dr. Tiffany Taft

Whoever said that being a woman was easy, was sharing alternative facts. My truth, being a woman sometimes is hard, but I love it. From the day we are born until our souls depart our body, there is something unique about every phase of our womanhood that is absolutely, undeniably, incredibly amazing. Every day, I am empowered and inspired by the women in my life that truly make it look so easy.

This chapter is personal for me as it shares my journey of challenges and real truths to understanding and knowing my body. I was forced to face some real unhappy truths and learn how to successfully navigate through each of them without holding onto a victim mentality. No, it was not easy. Yes, I often suffered alone, in silence, and wanted to give up, but I made it, and each challenge presented a story and a passion for me to live out my purpose. I hope that it will inspire you to want to know more about you, your body, and its divine feminine power as we take off the mask, dig deep into our truths, and speak out. Silence is no longer an option.

In this chapter, we seek to understand our bodies and ourselves through the perspective of our WOMBanhood, but like the title of this chapter, we are more than a womb. What is a womb you ask? This seems like such a simple and obvious answer. But is it really? Well, we will keep it simple here (insert smile). Webster defines the womb as "the lower part of the female body where offspring are conceived and gestate before birth." Seems simple enough, right? Every female is born with one (well, there are a few that are not, that's a story for another time) and in theory is also born with every egg she will ever have in life in the hope of one day, using them to create a legacy or two of her own. Our womb is the seat of pain, joy, love, hate, anger, frustration, fear, and life. As I aged over the years, my seat grew and expanded in ways that would have a very profound effect on my life based on good and bad decisions I made. Like so many women, I have found that I am not alone, and my stories are not unique but what is different is that I choose to share so that others may find an awareness, knowledge, and healing. I am a voice for those that cannot or choose not to speak their truth or their pain.

The statistics are staggering for women of color, like me, who are survivors of sexual traumas or abuse, and other conditions such as fibroids, infertility, diagnoses of cervical cancer, or loss of a child due to a miscarriage. For most women, when they dream of one day being able to conceive and birth children, they never factor in any of the crazy things mentioned above. Navigating what life throws at us and our female parts become a delicate balance, we must learn to overcome in a manner that serves our greater selves. It is important to maintain this balance should you decide to use the womb for pregnancy one day. Always remember to take care of you and your inner fitness first. So, with that, let the HEALING begin.

I was born the only child to my parents, who raised me in the south with Christian values. There's nothing like a praying mother! This was the best thing my mom could have ever given me. For all the years of good and bad that I would experience, no matter what, I always had my faith and God as my protector. I didn't have the model childhood, and yes there were many times that I questioned God over the years (crazy, who does that?) as to why my life was set up like it was. I had to remind myself constantly; He has a plan and to just be still.

From the very early age of six, I always knew that health and wellness would be "that thing" for me. A natural mix of east meets west medicine, and alternative therapies have been my go-to. For far too long, I leased out my own life, energy, and time to traditional forms of medicine that only treated the parts of me and not the WHOLE of me. I am now a womb care advocate because of my personal experiences, and I seek to use the bodies experiences to tell their stories and support women's health and well-being of the mind, body, and spirit. It is so ironic that one day many, many, years ago I had to take my own advice because my body was giving me so many physical messages that she was just not healthy and holding on by a thread.

At this stage of my life, I can look back and clearly see many detours that I took that I wish I had not. The elders say, "with time comes experience, healing, and forgiveness." This statement has been so true for me. Although I had a father present in the home, he was not present in my life. This would be a hurt that I would live with for years until I learned to change that narrative, have the hard conversations, and forgive him for me. Don't get it twisted; it took me years to get there. I experienced two devastating losses when I lost my sons (one at 14 months (my sunshine baby) and one miscarriage (my angel baby)). I felt like my body had failed me, and the thing I wanted most in life would never be for me. Now I hear you saying; you're not special. That has happened to me. You are right, but how we handle it is very different. You see for me because I have always had such a strong spiritual foundation, I have been able to keep my spirits high in even my darkest times. I have been broken, into pieces, but God made a way.

Never fear, my story and journey are not over, and none of it will ever define negatively, who I am as a woman. Our past experiences do not define us; they are life lessons, not life sentences. I am not stuck there, but if I had to be honest with myself, there are times I have thought, how different my life would have been with a few different lessons, interventions, or decisions. These lessons have shaped and given me a strength that would have broken many but has also provided the greatest space for the forgiveness of myself and those that I feel played a part in the hurt I felt. I was angry for a long time but had to realize that the anger was only hurting me and my womb. In addition to the loss of my children, I survived stage 4 cervical cancer and two large uterine fibroids (the size of a four-month pregnancy) that were located in the muscle walls of my uterus, that literally had me living like the walking dead. Through all of these physical situations, I remember tons of emotional stress just as equally painful and limiting my overall ability to heal myself. I wish that I had embraced more of the natural healing methods sooner so that I could have preserved my fertility. Despite all this loss, I have had an amazing life and am grateful for the lessons that led me to want to learn more and serve other women in a way that I can help them find their own path to wholeness and well-being.

How many times have you asked yourself, why me? I am a good girl. I have done everything right. I don't bother anyone. I stay in my lane. I am a good friend, good wife, good mother, good aunt, good sister, and more but for some reason, I have been chosen to NOT be able to do the one thing that women were created to do, be the vessel for which life flows. I stopped counting the number of times I asked that question. Who made that rule anyway? Who says that it's what we were made to do? Why is my life reduced to my body being objectified as a sexual object only capable of producing life, and I can't even do that? Stop! These are the things we tell ourselves and sabotage our happiness with because we don't understand how to fully remain in the present in the space of gratitude and abundance. So often we stay stuck with an emotional and spiritual mindset of lack. When I look back on my life, I can see a multitude of blessings and missed opportunities just to give praise and be grateful for what I had and experienced.

In order to permanently eliminate the negative mindset, we must first work on the mental cause of that way of thinking and figure out how to dissolve it. Proverbs 23:7 reads in part, "for as he thinketh in his heart, so is he." It all begins with a thought. Our thoughts become physical manifestations of our joy and fear. Our words have the power to give life or to hurt. I couldn't understand why I repeatedly had so many problems with my womb, low back, digestive system, and stress. It all started with my thoughts. The stories that I told myself over and over again that were not always ones that truly served my greater good. The manifestation was from anger, self-doubt, and unforgiveness. We don't always know where these thoughts come from or why we feel the way we do, which in itself, can make it difficult to know where to begin the healing. Have you ever just said to yourself, "if only I knew what was causing the pain, the hurt, the sadness, I could fix it." Believe it or not, we have all been there. Changing our thought patterns to produce a healthier mind-body connection is a must. Every muscle fiber in our body is made up of cells that store messages from our brain and tells us how to react and feel whether it is to protect us or to have us flee a situation. The unfortunate part is that so many women find themselves in a state of constant resentment, criticism, guilt, fear, regret, stress, anger, disappointment, lack, or more and that movie continues to be on repeat as we move through every phase of womanhood. The older we get, the more sophisticated the challenge becomes. The crazy part is that most of us also create these self-sabotaging moments that really can send us into a downward spiral.

Let this story encourage you to change the narrative that you, or others, have been telling you all your life. You ARE a Queen, a warrior, a strong woman, a game-changer, and an absolute gift to all mankind. Without you, creation would cease. I chose to change the narrative about me and my life, and I encourage you to find your PURPOSE and change your narrative too. I thank God every day for a new opportunity to get it right. I have learned that when your life falls apart, you either grow well or grow a tumor. A physical manifestation of the pain of your emotional self. As women, we internalize our voice, our pain. The pain and negative energy are kept in our womb or sacred space. This is the seat at which all life comes from, and all our emotions are kept. An unhealthy womb leads to a host of unhealthy life outcomes. The body is a mirror image of how we live and show up in our lives. The body speaks to us in whispers in the form of fatigue, anxiety, depression, aches or pains, irregular menses, fibroids, cancers in the body. We must be careful as to whom we chose to share our most sacred sensual gift of sexuality with as we carry those partners for up to seven years along with all those partners they may have had. I had to learn the hard way to not stay in situations that were not helping to grow and nurture me emotionally, mentally, or spiritually.

You can't go back and change the beginning, but you can start where you are and change the ending.

Here are just a few tips that I found helpful in my journey that may help you begin thinking about what plan will work best for you.

- Eliminate what does not serve you or help you to evolve. This requires a real and honest conversation with yourself and may take you some time, but the more you focus on you and what you need, the easier it becomes to say yes to you. This elimination may include people (family, friends, relationships) that you have had for years that may hurt to end but will be necessary to your thriving.

- Live fully in the moment. Live without regret and in service to others. It is important to find your purpose. That thing you were made to do that only you can do like no other. Every day I am grateful for my gifts and that I walk in a purpose and gifting that brings so much joy. The balance gets hard some days, but when I think about all the joy, it makes it worth every minute.

- Surround yourself with a tribe that gets you. Likeminded people that nurture you and your authentic self. This is key to your inner fitness.

Although scary, I am honored to share and be vulnerable enough so that you will see at least one thing in this story that resonates with you to be the change you need to live more fully. This thing called life is not easy to navigate and there are so many messages, tools, and guides, that it can all be overwhelming. Please know that this book was intentional. It was prayed for and over by every contributor. It was written with you in mind, and every story in every chapter is you or a woman you may know. Please share this work with the women in your inner circle so that you all may continue or start conversations that have been silent for too long. We are our sister's keeper.

I hope that by me sharing my story, and the transparency to open up my truths, you are blessed and encouraged to take the path and journey that is right for you. It is my purpose to educate and create awareness for women in a manner that serves them. I AM a woman in service to other women who seeks to inspire them to live well at every phase of womanhood. I understand all too well through my own stories how important it is to have a strong spiritual foundation and meaningful friendships and relationships, that sustain the mind, body, and soul. Womanhood is a beautiful title with much responsibility. Remember, though, you are a Queen, free, and hold the power to give life and change nations.

I live daily to become a more spiritual being having a human experience in the fullest possible way I can. I will continue to quiet the mind, so my soul may speak. Every day I AM living more fully, and I AM thriving.

I leave you with this daily gratitude prayer that will help you heal from the inside out:

Dear God, I thank you for every day you give me and the opportunity to be present fully in this life. I know at times I may seem ungrateful and resentful about how my life looks, but please know that it is the flesh of me that is weak. I thank you daily for your grace and mercy over my life and know that I could live forever and never fully repay you for all you have done for me and protected me from, seen and unseen.

About the Author

Dr. Tiffany H. Taft is a womb care advocate, focused on the education and research of the healing. Dr. Taft helps women use their body's experiences to tell their stories to support their mental, physical, and spiritual well-being. For years, Dr. Taft leased out her life, energy, and time to traditional forms of medicine that only treated the parts of her and not the WHOLE. Today she has proven system that helps women improve and preserve their own womb health naturally.

Dr. Taft is an author and speaker who inspires, educates, and empowers other women to live well at every phase of womanhood. Dr. Taft is licensed and certified in a full spectrum of integrative health therapies that support health and healing, including health nutrition coach, advanced yoga instructor, birth/postpartum doula, childbirth educator, esthetician, licensed massage therapist, aromatherapist, reflexologist and reiki master. She helps women restore their emotional, physical, and spiritual balance through evidence-based integrative therapies that support health and well-being of the WHOLE person. Finally, Dr. Taft is currently pursuing her B.S. in Nursing with a minor in Psychology and plans to continue her education toward completing her second Doctorate as a Nurse Practitioner (DNP) focusing her practice in the continuum of women's health and wellness needs, naturally.

Sacred Soul Wellness, LLC www.sacredsoulwellness.org
For inquiries email: Info@DrTiffanyTaft.com
Connect with Dr. Taft (FaceBook, Instagram, Twitter) @DrTiffanyTaft
LinkedIn @SacredSoulWellness

Power Booster #9
By Cathy Upshire

*"If God purposed you to bind up broken hearts,
don't waste your time trying to bind up those
who don't have one? They won't get "IT" or you."*

They that are whole need not a physician. Luke 5:31

- Cathy Upshire, *"Woman Find Thyself*

We can so easily find ourselves trying to prove our value to people who don't see it. And try as you may, they won't. People will recognize the value of a thing if it's going to bring value to *them*. Trying to sell a wheelchair to a room full of able-bodied people who have the full use of their legs is not only a waste of time; it's a waste of energy. No matter how large the discount or how passionate your pitch, they're not going to be convinced a wheelchair is going to bring value to them, because it won't. If you ride that chair into a room full of people who *don't* have the use of their legs, you won't have to say a *word*; they'll not only recognize the value it'll bring to their lives, they'll pay you every dime of what it's worth.

If you're discouraged because no one seems to value you or your gifts, perhaps you're in the wrong *room*, the wrong *relationship*, the wrong *church*, the wrong *company*, maybe even the wrong *town*.

And I'll end with this; a quote by Helen Schucman in her book, *A Course of Miracles, "Lord, where do you want me to go? What do you want me to say? To WHOM?"*

<u>Introspection</u>

Where does the Lord want you to go? Really think about it;
jot it down. What does he want you to say? What is a
common theme when you share something, you're
passionate about sharing? Really think about that; jot it
down. Now, who do you usually have in mind when you're
talking about it; when you're thinking about it? Really think
about that; jot it down. If you don't know, pray the prayer
in *"A Course of Miracles"* to find out.

About the Author

Cathy Upshire is a wholeness strategist, author, speaker, minister and wellness coach. She helps women who have lost their sense of identity and power to not only reclaim it so that they can live their lives with dignity and resolve, but she also helps them break free from the clenching jaws of their past. Cathy is the CEO and Founder of Broken Wings Coaching, LLC; an online coaching business. She takes women on their own personal journeys to wholeness, healing, authenticity, self-acceptance, and self-love. Cathy isn't a doctor or a therapist. She likens herself as a beautiful butterfly. The colors and intricate patterns of her wings represent all of the collective life experiences she's had and the many lessons she's learned along the way. Cathy spreads her wings proudly (void of shame); she spreads them wide because they legitimize her, they authenticate her, they are God's signature and seal that she is a transformed being; ready and suitable for the task at hand. Cathy is also a former Certified Crisis Advocate for victims of domestic violence and sexual assault.

Cathy holds a Bachelor's of Science Degree in Electronics Technology from DeVry University and has written two books: Woman Find Thyself and Evolution of a Woman. She is the mother of three adult children (Andre, Quincy, and Aja). Her son, Quincy, went on to be with the Lord on February 7, 2018 (he was 33 years old) but he continues to live on in her heart. Cathy lived in Chicago for 43 years but now reside in Louisville, KY.

Broken Wings Coaching, LLC www.CathyUpshire.com
For inquiries email cathyupshire@outlook.com
Connect with Cathy (FaceBook, Instagram and Twitter) @CathyUpshire

ACKNOWLEDGMENTS

The Thrive Girl Thrive movement is powered by our collective strength, glued together with love and lifted up by the grace of God. I want to thank the expert authors, Dr. Celeste Owens and Dr. Valeka Moore who said yes without hesitation and who believed in this project at its inception.

Special thank you to my amazing authors who entrusted their voices to me with open hearts. You are my heroes! And now the bonds that exist between us are forever etched in history.

Love,
Dr. Marsie

Made in United States
Orlando, FL
28 September 2023

37378707R00107